Beatrice's Ledger

BEATRICE'S LEDGER

*Coming of Age in the
Jim Crow South*

Ruth R. Martin WITH
Vivian B. Martin

THE UNIVERSITY OF
SOUTH CAROLINA PRESS

© 2022 University of South Carolina

Published by the University of South Carolina Press
Columbia, South Carolina 29208

www.uscpress.com

Manufactured in the United States of America

31 30 29 28 27 26 25 24 23 22
10 9 8 7 6 5 4 3 2 1

Library of Congress Cataloging-in-Publication Data
can be found at http://catalog.loc.gov/.

ISBN 978-1-64336-315-8 (hardcover)
ISBN 978-1-64336-316-5 (ebook)

Dedicated to Joe Robinson and Beatrice Hodges Robinson.
May their spirits inspire generations living and to come.

Contents

Illustrations

Acknowledgments

At 91, I have learned time and again that our major accomplishments are never possible without help from others. I started doing interviews and collecting materials for this project more than 20 years ago, but I started the work that produced this book several decades before that.

I often reflect in wonder at how good those Black teachers in segregated schools in South Carolina actually were. I think of them when a stray fact catches my attention and I remember where I first heard of it, somewhere back in my early school days. Today, it's common to hear people in public life strew grammatical errors throughout their speech—*him* where it should be *he; who* and *whom* often misplaced—causing me to ask, why is it that I, a poor Black girl from South Carolina, know the difference, and political leaders and TV broadcasters don't?

There were many people helping me know better, some of whom readers will meet in this book. Not just the community of educators and religious leaders but also aunts who sent hard-earned money from New York to help pay for my sister and me to attend high school. Aunt Anna's home nearby in South Carolina was a comfortable refuge, with decorative touches I hoped to own one day. Sometimes I think I hear her rocking chair.

In the late 1990s, I sought out members of my 1946 ninth-grade class at Johnsville-Simmons for oral history interviews. As a social work professor, I introduced oral history research into my discipline as a way to help students and practitioners better understand communities, their strengths and stressors. It made sense to start with oral history to better understand the times and how my classmates and I were able to succeed against the odds. I interviewed three of my ten classmates—Justine Stephens McCants, Thomas Warren, and Redell Stokes Fields—and had informal conversations with a couple of others. Only Redell, a retired educator living in Walterboro, South Carolina, and I remain from that graduating class. My husband Rutrell Martin, who died in 2005, drove me to those interviews in South Carolina, which he also did for other projects over the years.

Esther Simmons wrote a helpful letter explaining the role her grandfather played in offering and clearing the land for the Simmons School in 1887. My sister-in-law Cornelia Martin was often helpful with newspaper articles and programs from funerals of people we'd known for so long.

My brother F. D. came through with the big find: mother's ledger. The ledger factored in my first attempt to tell this story. In 2006, after my husband died, I took a continuing education memoir course at the University of South Florida that gave me confidence in my storytelling. It was a departure from the academic writing I'd learned to squeeze myself into for so many years.

In recent years, aid came from surprising places. I am grateful to Ray Thomas, a lifelong resident of Smoaks. I did not know him while growing up but was well aware of the Thomas family. We connected through another contact I made during research; Ray knew my family and even recalled coming to the gristmill my father ran. In an act of kindness, Ray looked up a record at the county clerk office and clarified other information about property that my father purchased from one of his relatives.

I was introduced to Ray via email by Dr. James Connor, a retired pediatrician living in California. Jim Connor grew up in Smoaks, up the road from my family. He's a few years older than I and did not remember me, but like the Thomases, the Connors were another white family along the road with whom we worked and interacted throughout my youth. Rallie Liston, a school superintendent who is a generation removed from the Listons with whom my siblings and I played, was a delight.

I pushed forward, despite stretches of procrastination, for many years, not sure where the book was going. I am sure there were people who just thought I should give it up already. Getting the manuscript into the hands of Dr. Ehren Foley, acquisitions editor at the University of South Carolina Press, was a blessing I wish for all authors who are toiling over such a labor of love. The professionalism, promptness, and respect with which he handled the submission was astounding. He understood the work right away. From the reviewers to production editor, the cover designer, copyeditor, and marketing staff, the team got behind the book in a way that was inspiring.

Dana Chandler, archivist at Tuskegee, came through with an image that speaks to my memories of the "line of march" I endured but came to appreciate at Tuskegee. The South Carolina Department of Archives and History deserves acknowledgement for its stewardship of materials, including images such as the insurance photos of my elementary school, in a manner more technologically advanced than can be found in many states. The professionals who maintain these databases provide a record of people, places, and events that, as contemporary politics illustrate, can be too quickly forgotten.

The major support without which I could not have completed this project is my family, my adult children, all of whom played some role. My son Rutrell Yasin, a writer, did an early reading of a partial manuscript (ca. 2009), while my daughter Sonya Martin Bornheimer was often available to help prepare the manuscript. Valerie Martin set up a reading—a performance, actually—of the first chapter during a Black History event at the agency where she works. The reception was encouraging and helped me to push forward. Anthony Martin, a retired Army officer in his second career as an historical archaeologist, helped me understand the presence of German POWs in South Carolina. Maxine Martin did a lot of the note-taking and transcribed raw materials throughout the years. Vivian Martin, a journalism professor and my collaborator, helped me discover how pieces of my life connected to bigger stories, and helped me tell those stories, pushing for more information and work when I wanted to stop. When I lost my eyesight and a stroke caused other complications, Vivian brought the project home. I am grateful for my family and the many others who helped lift me up and supported me along the way. As the gospel song by Albert A. Goodson (1956) goes, "We've come this far by faith."

Ruth R. Martin
Hartford, Connecticut
November 27, 2021

PROLOGUE

It was not a school day, so I was enjoying time with Mama and Papa as we stood under the walnut tree that was about two hundred feet north of our house. The tree was no more than twenty feet from the main dirt highway that ran through our property. Not far from where we stood, the wooded area began. Far to the right was the Risher family's land, on which stood a field of asparagus. The Rishers had given Papa permission to help himself to it whenever he wished. He was the only one in our family who liked asparagus. I don't think the Risher family liked asparagus either, because only once did I see the women of the family gather any.

Papa and Mama were chuckling about that when we heard a car door slam in front of the house. A car engine started up again, and we saw a black Ford heading in our direction. The car stopped, and two people got out and headed to where we stood. One was a white man of medium frame and approximately 5'10" tall. The woman, also white, was a little heavy and perhaps 5'5" tall. Looking back, I don't recall if his car was marked "Sheriff," but at eleven years old I did know he was someone with authority. They came over and greeted Papa.

"Hey, Joe, how you doing?"

"Fine, suh."

The lady spoke, "Joe."

My father seemed to know her and greeted her. "Good evening, Miz Thomas."

The man then began to speak. "Joe, we seem to have a problem here. Miz Thomas seems to think you owe money to her husband, and she is here to collect it."

As the conversation went on, I grew more afraid for Papa. By that point in my life I had heard many nightly discussions between my parents and other adults about things that happened to colored people. I once heard Papa and Cousin Jeemes (James Simmons) discuss the story of how two Black men accused of some infraction—I heard only that they ran through some white family's backyard—were tied to the back of a buggy and made to run behind the buggy until they collapsed, and then were dragged to their death.

Beatrice (Mama) and
grandchild, late 1940s.

Those stories drove my fear for Papa that day. But Papa's expression did not
mirror the same fear that I was experiencing. He actually appeared calm, as if
he were in the right. But even as a young girl, I knew being in the right did not
mean that a Black man would not be harmed.

I grabbed our fat white puppy and walked a short distance away, careful not
to make any move that would call attention to myself or cause the white man and
woman to react angrily. My father must have told them that he could prove what
he said because he told my mother, "Bea, bring the book." He always called her
Bea, pronounced "Bee," for Beatrice. Mother left, walking at a fast pace through
the path and into the house (see photo 1). The man continued to talk to Father;
Miz Thomas stood by still fired up, insisting she was in the right.

As dangerous as it was in those days to call a white person a liar, my father
kind of smiled graciously, saying, "No, ma'am. I settled my debts with Mr. Rommie."

My ears perked up when I heard the name Rommie. I had been hearing my
family refer to him for as many years as I could remember. Someone was going
to Mr. Rommie to hoe or pick cotton. I had never seen him but imagined him to
be an elderly white man. My father sometimes went to Mr. Rommie's house and
came back with a ham or some seeds to plant, or whatever seemed to be needed.
In later years I learned Mr. Rommie owned a grocery store, but I was not up on
all that at eleven years old.

My siblings and I had had a good laugh a year or two earlier when one of Mr. Rommie's relatives, a woman, wrote my father an awkwardly worded postcard that read, "Joe Robinson, see hear. I have some beans at the Yancey Place need picking. Come and pick them right away."

Papa chuckled as he said, "I don't owe her one dime." But the tone of the card, demanding, was no joke. In the end, Papa sent his older children to "help her out."

That afternoon as I watched fearfully, Papa stood unwavering. Mama returned as quickly as she could from the house. She was holding an oblong gray book. She walked up to my father, book in hand, opened it, and pointed to an entry. He said to Mama, "Show them the book."

The sheriff and the woman both spent some time looking in the book. He then looked down at the woman, and they had a spirited conversation. She finally nodded. He made some comment to Papa, which seemed to vindicate him. They left without a word of apology from her. At eleven I knew that when one is wrong, it is courteous to apologize, but I also already knew that this did not apply when it came to whites in South Carolina in the early forties. Whatever was in that book, I knew it was important and that my parents knew the value of keeping records as proof of transactions. It was more than seventy years later before I learned what those records revealed about how hard my parents worked for our family.

one

BEATRICE'S LEDGER

I had been anticipating its arrival for several days. My brother Fred Douglas (F. D.) told me he was putting Mama's book in overnight mail, but this was the longest overnight I had ever experienced. He found the book while going through Mama's trunk, where she kept many old papers. Mama had been dead for thirty-eight years. Other family members had moved into the house. F. D. had now returned to South Carolina and lived some ninety miles away from Smoaks. In 2002 he cleared out Mama's old trunk, which was still in a closet in the family house. He was aware that I was now collecting materials from our past. When he came across the journal, he telephoned me in Connecticut, excited.

"Hey, my favorite sister!" he greeted me. (It was a standing joke that we used because I was his only sister still alive.) "Guess what I just found?"

I played along and asked, "What have you found, ol' brother of mine?"

"Mama's old book, and it has a whole lot of old bills and stuff stuck in the pages. I thought you might want it."

"Really?" I asked. "You are not talking about that old book from way back when? You mean it is still around?"

F. D. assured me that he was holding it in his hands and could send it to me through overnight mail. I was giddy with excitement when I first held that book from so many years past in my unsteady hands. I rushed to tear off the priority-mail cover.

At first glance, I was disappointed. "This is not Mama's journal! This is old and tattered!"

On closer examination, I saw that the book appeared to be the same size as the one I remembered. It was gray, but much darker than I remembered. In the front center was the word "LEDGER" printed in uppercase letters. Ahh, I mused, it had not been a book Papa referred to that day long ago, but a ledger. Despite the ledger being tattered, the strings hanging from it were strong, almost cloth-like (see photo 2).

Beatrice's ledger.

I slowly opened the pages while allowing my mind to wander back to the first time I became aware of this ledger, the fearful day that a sheriff, most likely employed by the county, visited with a local white woman to help her collect a debt. I never knew what was in the book that had caused the sheriff and woman to back off from the initial demand, but I knew it was something the sheriff deemed credible enough to halt further collection efforts.

What was in that book?

I began to thumb through the ledger. It was a widely used model, No. 476, from S. E. & M. Vernon in New York, which made journals and ledgers up into the 1960s. As I have gathered from examples for sale on eBay, the books have practical information on the inside and back pages much like an almanac. In our copy there was useful information for farmers, such as "Quantity of Seed Required to Plant an Acre"—Corn, sugar, 10 quarts; Oats, 2 bushels—general information ("Business Law in Everyday Use), and postal information with the date, as in March 1922 (First Class mail 5 cents for up to a pound). The facing pages inside had rows and columns to allow for double-entry bookkeeping for line-by-line transactions.

My parents used the ledger to document a variety of activities. The first entry listed above the top margin read "The Setting up of the Lovely Hill Ladies Court 1930." A number of entries record the minutes of this group, for which Beatrice Robinson is listed as president. Entries indicate that Mama would call the meeting to order and sing the old hymn "Come to Jesus." The group collected dues of $1.50 from farm families, a fee paid in increments, mainly quarterly, throughout the year. Touchingly, the minutes list payments given to members during difficult times. The Ladies Court gave my aunt Anna B. Harrison, vice president of the group, a dollar during a difficult time and paid "Sister Beatrice Robinson" a dollar to help after "house burn" in 1930.

I did not know anything about that crisis, for I was not yet born, but I do know the ledger itself weathered many a storm, from our house burning down in 1934, to our move to the pole house in 1934, to our move in 1939, to our house burning down in 1941, to our move in 1941, to Father's death in 1942, and on and on. This ledger deserved a salute for perseverance. I saw that many pages had been torn out over the years when there was a need for a sheet of paper to write a note, a grocery list, and sometimes a letter. Although many of the 188 pages were torn out, the ledger still showed examples of my father's entrepreneurial activities sawing lumber, grinding corn, and grinding rice. It was missing many pages, but in some ways it told too much.

What I wanted to know from the ledger at that moment was what happened the day the sheriff came with the white woman to demand that my father pay up. Now, after all those years, I was going to learn what they saw in this ledger on the day I was so afraid Papa might be killed. I was not certain what I was looking for, so I was forced to read each page. Finally, on page 120, above the margin in Mother's handwriting was recorded "Paid Mr. Rommie Thomas," and below the margin was the following entry:

Corn	1 bu.
Cash	125
owe him three	3.00

My memory was that Papa and Mr. Rommie did much business together, and the ledger confirms this. Although Mama did not use every cell of the ledger left to right as a professional bookkeeper might, she recorded all the dates and money owed and paid. Phrases like "Three hands" (three people) and "Work out the same" (even exchange) might confuse at first glance, but it was language that the sheriff understood.

May—Got $4.00 in cash,	*Work out the same.*	*3 hands 1 day and 3 days.*
1935-8	Joe Robinson owe Mr. Rommie Thomas	3.00
	Paid Cash	1.25
1936-12	paid corn	1 bu.
	paid corn	1bu
1936	Got of Mr. Rommie	one bu. 3pk wheat.
	Paid on the wheat	½ bu of clean rice
	Got peanuts 1 bu of Mr. Rommie	Paid for same in work
May 8	Paid in hoeing	$2.00
June	Got meat and lard	.30 each.

Hoe out $2.00 more work. At this time Settlement here with Mr. Rommie Thomas & Joe Robinson not to come up any more.

There is a break in the pages. Pages 121 and 122 are torn out, apparently to fill a need for some paper. The ledger picks up again for the year 1939 above the top margin (see photo 3). Below the line Mother recorded:

	Rommie Thomas to Joe Robinson,	One Joe Robinson hoed 5 acres of cotton and 3 acres of rice.
	Got of Mr. Rommie this time $2. on the cotton,	1.25 one time, .35 one time.
	picking this cotton 3 hands 2 days,	haven't received anything yet.
1940	hoe other, Mr. Rommie sick, 2 weeks & 4 days in hand over to the Yancy place.	1.4 days received 9½ lbs. of meat and one puppy.
	Picked this same cotton.	3 hands 2 days received $1.34.

7

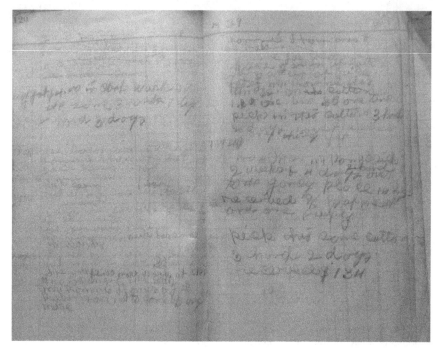

Page from Mama's ledger showing transactions
between my father and Rommie Thomas.

I was amazed to learn that Papa got us the fat white puppy as part of a settlement with Mr. Rommie. I could not have imagined Papa paying for a puppy.
F. D. later clarified this for me by explaining the puppy was a bulldog.

Most important, through the ledger I see my hardworking parents struggling
to make a living for their family. I see my father paying his debts. I see them
not being too proud to do what needed to be done to feed their family, even to
barter. I see me, the frightened child that day, who saw her parents jump another
hurdle in their lives and didn't let that stop them from moving on to the next
challenge. My strong, resilient parents, who never failed to tell and show us by
making sure that we went to school: "Education is your way out."

I reviewed what I had written and concluded, "That is not too bad." Yet
something was troubling me. I had certainly stuck to the facts as I knew them.
So I decided to call my brother. "F. D., do you remember when the white lady
came to the house with that white man to collect money she said Papa owed her
husband?"

"No, I don't remember that."

Right away, I knew what I wanted to know the answer to. "When did Mr. Rommie die?"

The answer to this would clear up several things for me. Mama wrote in her ledger, "Mr. Rommie is sick." This was in 1940. Also, she showed payments made to them by Rommie Thomas for picking the same cotton they had hoed.

I asked F. D., "When was cotton picking time in South Carolina?"

"September to October, if it's a late cotton crop."

I knew my need was to test my memory to authenticate Mama's ledger and to learn more about when Mr. Rommie died. This was important because it also gave me a sense of the age of everyone. My search of the 1930 census did not show Rommie Thomas. After a week of inquiry, F. D. telephoned me with the name and address of someone he had seen over the weekend who lived next door to the Thomases growing up. Although she did not remember Rommie Thomas, she knew the family.

"If you go look in Green Pond Methodist Cemetery, you will find them all buried there."

"How will I know? Do they have tombstones?"

"Sure. They were rich. The ones who lived next door to us lived in a big white house and owned a grocery store."

She gave me the names of three of her cousins who were siblings and older than she, who knew the answer, and suggested I ask the brother first. He was Brinton Edwards, who became one of the first decorated soldiers to enter the military from around home. Brinton gave me Rommie's wife's name, Bessemer, and his two brothers' names, Arthur and Joseph. I used this information to search the cemetery tombstones on the internet and finally to locate the person I assumed was Rommie.

Darn it! Why did so many people in the South use nicknames? His given name was not Rommie, but Herbert J.

Finally, F. D. gave me the name of Nine Drain, who grew up near us in a family I will tell you about later.

Nine had enough information to help me locate the family in the 1930 census. Sure enough, there was Herbert with his family, and the son, Milton, who Nine said was his friend. In *The Census of Death Reports,* I finally found the information I was searching for: Rommie Thomas (Herbert J.) died in October 1940. His wife would have tried to collect the debt soon after that. Mom's ledger was authenticated. I was able to understand what had been a puzzle. I knew Mama's ledger would be an important companion as I looked back on the past.

two

SMOAKS

Smoaks, South Carolina, where I come from, is in the lowcountry of the state, an eighty-mile car ride northwest from Charleston, at the junction of US 21 and SC 64. To understand its place in history, Smoaks has to be scooped up with all the other rural towns that constitute Colleton County (formerly St. Bartholomew's Parish) around the basin of the three rivers that made this land so fertile for rice plantations prior to the Civil War. Colleton reportedly had the highest concentration of plantations in South Carolina, where slaves toiled in the mosquito-laden heat to produce the industry that built many fortunes. Branchville, eleven miles from Smoaks, touts itself as having the world's first railroad junction, built in 1828 and running from Charleston to Branchville. There is beauty among the palmettos, but the romanticism for which some now pursue plantation weddings and luxury resorts would have been lost on many of us living there in the 1930s and 1940s.

The Sanborn Fire Insurance Map for 1930, the year I was born, shows a central section with the obligatory post office, general stores, doctors' offices, agricultural storage, and related businesses. We lived on the outskirts, among farms and some lands that had not been tilled since the prior century.

Smoaks claims 1789 as its establishment date. It has a couple of origin stories, although they are not mutually exclusive. The area was formerly known as Smokes X (Cross) Road, reportedly a campfire and central meeting place for settlers from the surrounding countryside, who helped protect one another from pirates hiding in the woods to rob people as they crossed the Edisto River. The other part of the origin story is that Smoaks is derived from the German family name of two brothers who came to the country to fight in the Revolutionary War and were awarded land for their service. Their family name, Rauch, is German for Smoke. According to some accounts, the family name went through different spellings—Smoakes, Smoke, Smoaks—because of intentional changes or misspellings through history.[1] To me, it is Smoaks, the place of my birth and, if all goes to plan, my final resting place.

I was born there in 1930. Although I grew up with the knowledge that I was born on November 25, it was not until I graduated from high school and applied for and received my birth certificate that I learned my recorded birthday was late October. My mother was certain that my birthday was in November, and when I went to New York and shared the information with my mother's sister, Aunt Minnie, she corroborated my mother's version. "No, honey," she enlightened me. "I know you were born in November, because I delayed my move to Washington, D.C., until after Thanksgiving because I was waiting for my sister to give birth to you." There was often a gap in time between births and their official recording, especially of rural Black births, making such discrepancies common. I was delivered by Anna Jackson, the midwife who delivered most of the Black babies in those years, even as midwives were coming under more regulation and getting pushed out of their role. I assume she would have recorded the birth when she went into town, possibly along with the names of others she had delivered.

Because of the mix-up, I have used two birthdays. For work and official purposes, I use the October date, and for my celebrations, I use November. If someone gets confused and sends a gift in October, I can always let her know to remember my birthday in November as well. That way I can get two for one. I am not the only "doubly advantaged" person from my community. Redell Stokes Fields, a classmate from my earliest years, recently mentioned the discrepancy between her misrecorded official birthday and the one recognized by her family when she was interviewed for a newspaper article about her ninetieth birthday.[2]

My mother's ledger complicates it a bit more because she lists my birth year as 1931. It would make me a year younger than I spent my life believing; 1930 seems more likely. She also misrecorded my brother F. D.'s birth by a year. The birth listings were not contemporaneous, possibly explaining the errors. Papa's death is misrecorded as well. Mama got most things right, but these entries leave me puzzled.

I was the seventh and last child in the family. My father, Joe Robinson, married Blanche Rasberry, who died in childbirth, leaving three children: Woodrow, Mattie Mae, and Joe Junior. He then married my mother, Beatrice Hodges, who gave birth to four children: Henrietta, Madison (Matt), Fred Douglas (F. D.), and me, Ruth (no middle initial). Mama eventually decided that because I didn't have a middle name, we should choose one. She was pleased with herself when she chose the name Ruth Ash because it was her sister-in-law's name. That name didn't work because my family and the Simmons girls began calling me Ruth Ass. I eventually took the middle name Vivian, although I do not recall why.

My family wasted little time nicknaming me "Baby." I detested the name. It stuck with me even as an adult. I was about twenty-six and walking down Sutter Avenue from the post office, near where I lived on Herzl Street in Brooklyn, when a fair-complected man driving down the street in the opposite direction yelled, "Hey, Baby." When I ignored him and kept walking, he turned his car around and drove up alongside me. "Baby, don't you know me? I'm Elzera." Once I got over my initial fear, I saw it was a hometown boy from Smoaks whom I had not seen in years.

My nickname aside, I was known to assert myself from a very young age. I could read and write early, and Mama encouraged my growth in these areas. But my smart mouth went beyond the classroom and academics. A dean at Voorhees, where I boarded for my junior year in high school, told Henrietta, my sister, who also attended Voorhees, that Leola Edwards and I were "the two meanest girls to ever come from Smoaks" and told my mother there was as much difference between Henrietta and me as day and night. That was probably not a surprise. The old folks back home used to say, "Ruth is as sassy as a blacksnake." My view was that I was only standing up for myself—and that old people were not always right. It is a good thing I did not stick around to build a life within the constraints of South Carolina.

After all these years I am still ambivalent about the state where I was born. South Carolina, along with Mississippi, is often synonymous with the worst of life in the segregated South, even with the burgeoning tourism at Hilton Head and Myrtle Beach, which excluded Black people in my day. Although there were joyous times being around family in my childhood, whenever South Carolina turns up in the news, usually as the result of some tragic racist act, such as the church shooting in Charleston or some backward political decisions, I shake my head in quiet reminiscence and disgust, grateful that I was able to escape.

Possibilities for Black people were not that apparent in my youth. The state had a highly elaborated "Negro Law" starting in 1740 to control the enslaved and free people of color long before the Civil War.[3] After the war, South Carolina immediately began enacting Jim Crow laws restricting the movement of Black people in public places, limiting access to schools, and keeping Blacks from voting. Historian Terence Finnegan, who compared lynchings in Mississippi and South Carolina, noted that the former had more, but this was partly a result of South Carolina's Jim Crow laws allowing for more legal executions and other harsh treatment.[4] Whites in Mississippi had to improvise, so to speak.

Growing up as a "colored" girl in South Carolina in the 1930s and 1940s meant there were written and unwritten rules to navigate to avoid the wrath of whites: speak when spoken to; remember to say "Yes, ma'am" or "No, ma'am" or "Yes, sir" and "No, sir"; and make sure that it didn't sound too educated. The flatter it sounded the better—for example, "Noosuh" or "Yaasuh." Stick to your own schools, associate with your own kind, don't look us directly in the eyes but avert your eyes downward, step aside and allow us to pass, and on and on.

My mother sometimes said, "Smoaks did so many mean, cruel, dirty things. It will never grow any bigger." Strictly speaking, she wasn't wrong. The census counted 176 people in 1930, spiking from 132 in 1920, but estimated 116 in 2020, a trend similar to other small towns in the region. I never questioned what cruel, mean, and dirty things she meant. During those days, children sat quietly while the older folks discussed many issues. There was only the one sitting room. Even if parents wanted to, it would have been difficult to prevent children from hearing, even when parents spoke low, but children knew not to interrupt old folks or intervene in their discussion.

One event that seemed to be imprinted on the town was a double lynching (the local white press called it that) from 1909 that happened right in Smoaks. I did not know the specifics, but I grew up hearing enough indirect references to the horror that it seemed more contemporary than it was. As I learned while collecting information for this book, the lynchings made newspapers in several states, putting Smoaks on the map. The terrible events started on May 29, 1909, when J. Benjamin Smoak, the son of a prominent family, was shot in the chest by robbers as he was closing the family country store, J. L. Smoak & Son, near Smoaks Xroads. The robbers, who got away with cash and checks, were quickly identified as Frank Samuels and Acquilla "Quillie" Simmons, who, according to local newspaper reports, had "bad reputations" even prior to the tragedy. For a fee of $25 paid by Smoak's father, a young Black man followed the duo and witnessed them dividing the cash and burying the checks in a barn. The arm of the law, extended by active assistance from the father, brought in the two men, held an inquest, and convened a jury of white men well-known in the community, who found Samuels and Simmons guilty.

The justice system seemed to be moving in line according to due process (for the era), but as the constable left Smoaks to take the men to the county jail in Walterboro on June 11, they were besieged by a mob that news reports claim silently grew to 250–500 men, some from Orangeburg and Bamberg, through the night. The mob took the men back to the area where the armed robbery and murder had occurred and reportedly confronted them with a few questions, with some reports indicating that two other people were rounded up but released. The mob hanged the men in small pine trees, at which the mob began firing their guns, riddling the bodies with gunshots. In a page-one article headlined "DOUBLE LYNCHING AT SMOAKS. J.B. SMOAK'S MURDERERS CAUGHT AND KILLED.

FRANK SAMUELS AND ACQUILLA SIMMONS VICTIMS," the *Press and Standard* (June 16, 1909), the main local paper, based in Walterboro, began its account:

> Friday evening at 11 o'clock the citizens of the quiet community of Smoaks were startled by the report of volleys from at least one hundred guns, and they knew that the murderers of J. Benjamin Smoak had paid the penalty for their crime with their lives. The next morning's light revealed the form of Frank Samuels and Quillie Simmons tied to two small pine trees a few yards from the rail road track where it emerges into the woods about three hundred yards from the store of J.L. Smoak & Son.

The *Times and Democrat,* based in Orangeburg, similarly ran verbatim testimony from the coroner's jury, as well as a report headlined "Double Lynching. Two Negroes Hanged and Riddled with Shot."[5] Nobody in the mob was ever held to account for his participation in the murders, according to the newspaper reports. There is no doubt that such an event would have shocked even as it reaffirmed fears, and this certainly explains why it was alluded to in my day, though never recounted explicitly. The documented event and all of its horror, even when read about in 2019, makes more probable some of the other events that I heard remnants of over the years.

Even without specifics, children knew or intuited the need to not ask too many questions early, for their survival. When the bus with the white children passed us as we trudged to school, we never questioned why white children rode the bus and Black children walked. We recognized that the society we grew up in had informal and formal systems that dictated Black and white interactions. We were as separated as could be in schools, churches, restaurants, libraries, bathrooms, or when trying on clothes in the stores. When Blacks purchased goods, whites would not touch their hands while giving change but instead would place it on the counter. (Years later on a visit, as I waited for change after buying fish, I was almost shocked to see people still did this. "God," I said to myself, "I forgot this archaic ritual." I was so sorry I had already bought the fish, but felt like I was between a rock and a hard place. Raise a fuss and endanger those with me, or suck it up. I chose the latter.)

We played with some of these white youths after school, in my case Ann, Cornelia Ruth, and Mary Evelyn, and also visited in their homes. My brothers played ball with Sunny Liston, Terry Liston, and James Connor. Connor, a retired pediatrician and medical researcher who was in his nineties and living in California when I made contact with him, recalled his joy while playing or hunting with Blacks who lived around him. The world of Smoaks he remembers was one in which his family hired Blacks and lent money to them, and I recall some of this. He did not remember me—he was several years older—but says that the racial prejudice and slurs of those days were not part of his home life. Later he would realize that some of what he had simply viewed as "custom" was part of a systematic structure to disempower Blacks. He came to understand, for example, that his uncle, whom he saw lend hundreds of dollars to a Black farmer at the same time each year, did so because Blacks could not get loans at the local bank.

Blacks and whites navigated in and out of one another's lives carefully, but in some interactions there was a sense of shared humanness. My father sat and talked with white men for hours. Some of these men did business at his sawmill. These white men never entered our home, yet when they all sat around talking, some of what they told him was chilling.

Papa once shared how one of his white associates described the night he and a group of white men were attempting to catch a Black man for something for which he was presumed guilty (I do not recall ever knowing what that was). The Black man ran into the swamp. The group surrounded the swamp and waited for him to come out. The white man told my father that the Black man came up near him and made eye contact, and he allowed the man to crawl out of the swamp right beside him. Neither of them uttered a word. When daylight came, everyone else was surprised that the man was not in the swamp.

Papa told that story with complete faith that it would not be repeated. I am certain the man who told him the story had faith that my father would not repeat the story. Papa died before my twelfth birthday, and this is the first time I am telling this story. The man who told my dad the story is long dead, but in deference to his children or grandchildren who may still be alive, and out of respect for Papa and his informant, I will say no more.

three

MAMA AT THE POLE HOUSE

We moved to the pole house in 1934 after the home I was born in burned down. One of my earliest memories is of being thrown in a hole, away from the flames, and then later riding in a wagon alongside my mother to the new home. The fire could have started from any of a number of things—a log rolling off the fire, sparks from the chimney, wind fanning the fire—but I never heard any discussion about it. I had forgotten much about the size of the new home until some sixty-five years later, when my brother and I, along with our spouses, visited the site. Imagine the feeling of standing on soil your feet have not touched in such a long time. A lifetime of living flashed before my eyes as I saw the windows of the world through the eyes of a youngster. My brother and I took photographs with my 35-mm camera and RCA camcorder while our spouses looked on. Though now overgrown with pine trees, the site seemed to offer up memories of what had been there when we arrived in 1934.

We called it a pole house because it was made of medium-sized poles rather than huge split logs. Abraham Lincoln's house was a log cabin. We called ours a pole house. It was a four-room house with two bedrooms, a sitting room, and a kitchen. There was an entrance into the sitting room around the side from which we entered the first time I came to the house. We entered a hall that held a seating couch from which we sometimes entertained and that sometimes served as my bed. Mama and Papa's bedroom was to the left of this hall. Down the end of the hall was the second bedroom. It was large enough to hold two beds.

My siblings and I shared this room, boys in one bed and girls the other (sometimes three in each). The house was built high enough off the ground that we children could crawl under it and sit upright with room to spare over our heads. This was our play area. We did not have money for toys, so we built our own out of the materials of everyday life. Corn silk from a corncob became hair for dolls, old sardine cans became cars, and if we wanted wheels, we made do with spools of thread or used corncobs. We also made our own checkerboards and used bottle caps as checkers.

The sitting room did not have a chimney but a heater, a huge fifty-gallon oil drum. A door with hinges was cut into one side of the drum, which served for putting wood into the heater. Another round hole was cut into the top, through which a flue was inserted and extended through the roof of the house to carry out the smoke. It served to heat the whole house. Our yard was spacious. On the edge of the yard sat a huge persimmon tree that we kids enjoyed climbing. To the back of the house, about seventy-five feet away, was a large pear tree, and next to it was a grape vine. The house sat about a hundred feet from the road.

Some of the best of times, in what I now know was the poorest of times, took place in that tiny four-room house. Friends and relatives were always around, as were men working around Papa's sawmill. On Saturdays, people came with their corn and rice to be ground at Papa's rice and grist mill. Our move to the pole house made it easier to attend Simmons School, the only school for Black children in the area. We were now nearer to a predominantly Black ("colored") community). The Drain family was on our right and were regulars in our lives. Our neighbors to our left were James and Celie Simmons and their four children.

I came to really know Mama while we lived in the pole house. I don't remember when I put a face to the voice and kind things she did to take care of me. The memory of her doing things with and for me are as strong as the fresh smell of spring and of gardenias in the breeze, fresh pine needles, hot chocolate, sweet potato pies, and parch peanuts. She was Mama until I reached tenth grade and began calling her Mother. Somehow I got the notion that the word "Mother" was more encompassing than "Mama." I began calling her Mother, and F. D. joined with me. I don't know how I thought that any name would be sufficient to convey her care and role in my life. Like the day I stood in the sitting room of the pole house with my back to the fire. Mama looked in from the kitchen, saw my clothes on fire, quickly made it to me, grabbed some loose clothes off the chair, and smothered the flames. I hadn't realized I was on fire.

Who but Mama would include our names when we churned butter? Mama would skim the cream from the milk a day or so after the cows had been milked. The milk was in a big pail. After enough cream was skimmed and saved—and only Mama knew when it was enough—she placed it all in a quart jar, screwed the lid on tightly, held each end of the jar in her hands, and began to shake it. She would switch from shaking the jar to sitting down and lightly beating the jar against her knees. She made up a little song: "Come butter come, come butter come, Ruthie's at the gate, waiting for a little piece of cake cake cake, now come butter come." She then allowed us to take turns as the names changed, and before long we could see the cream turning to butter.

Little by little I put a face with that slow, soft-spoken, alto voice. I came to recognize her slender face; kind, deep-set brown eyes; medium-brown complexion; shoulder-length hair; and warm, gentle hands. She stood approximately 5'6" tall, with laughter in her voice. She was not a heavyset woman, but of medium weight. Years later I noted she was a bit hippy. Always she was with her pipe. If she ran out of her favorite Country Gentleman tobacco, she was irritable. We never wanted Mama to be without her tobacco or a pipe. If her pipe was damaged or the pipe stem was cracked or clogged, we improvised until she got a new pipe. We used a corncob and inserted a hole in the side of it, and cut bamboo canes found along by the ditch to make pipe stems.

Late in life, Mama gave up smoking. She was a passenger in a pickup truck accident and was forced to crawl out through the window. She was not seriously hurt, but along with the accident went her desire for her pipe. We visited her one Christmas, and I brought her a supply of tobacco. We were surprised to learn she no longer smoked.

Mama attended Claflin Normal School in Orangeburg, forerunner of the historically Black college. She and her half-brother Virgil were both students. Finances forced her to forgo her final year. Normal schools were created to train high school graduates to be teachers. Mama taught in her early years despite not finishing normal school. As the family came, she left teaching to raise us.

I have images of my mother out near the well teaching us games: "Ring around the Rosie," "How Many Miles to Barton's Bridge?," dodgeball, walking tall on sticks as clowns do today, and walking the barrel (this involved taking a one-hundred-gallon drum, which had contained gas that my dad bought to run his mills, and laying it on its side to climb on top, stand, balance, and roll with our feet, keeping it in a straight line). Sometimes we would stand on each side of the house and throw a ball across the top. The trick was to keep it going without touching the ground, similar to the game of volleyball. She taught us hopscotch and, before I started school, played tic-tac-toe with me.

Mama spent a lot of quality time with us. I benefited most because I spent many days alone with her before I started school. She served as our librarian, entertainer, playmaker, supporter, doctor, and conscience. One of her favorite sayings was "If your conscience doesn't condemn you, God won't." Mother made most situations teachable moments. When F. D. and I came in from playing in the road and announced that we wished we could find ten dollars, Mother explained, "If you were to find ten dollars, it would mean someone else lost it and that person may have needed it worse than you for a number of reasons: to put food on his family's table, to buy medicine for a sick child, to buy shoes for his children, and many other reasons." That was Mother the Spoiler. How could we continue to wish to find money when she had just put the burden of caring about someone else on our shoulders?

She had a range of sayings to keep us in line. "Feed the devil with a long spoon" was her way of teaching us to stay clear of troublemakers. We interpreted "Be careful when your hand is in the lion's mouth" to mean "When someone is against you, be gentle." And finally, she would say, "I know a snake when I see his tail," to which my brother Madison responded, "Yes, but you can tell him by his head best."

One day my mother left F. D. and me home with instructions to shop from the grocery truck. She gave us a note specifying what she wanted us to buy. Our form of payment was the eggs we were expected to give the grocery man. Before Mama left, she showed us one cracked egg, which she knew the truck driver would not take. We had a different idea. We decided to glue the cracked egg, trade it off to the truck driver, and use the money to purchase what we wanted. So we put the cracked egg in the basket along with the others. To our chagrin, the truck man examined every egg. When he came to the cracked egg, he calmly posed a question that also served as a statement: "I'm sure your Mama didn't mean for you to put this one in here?" We could only look sheepish without responding. We at least had the good graces to tell Mama when she came home. Her response: "You didn't think he would notice that was a cracked egg?" What better way to let us know that we were not smart? That was Mama in her subtle way, letting us know we had done something stupid and unethical.

Mother quoted from Booker T. Washington, Shakespeare, W. E. B. Du Bois, Langston Hughes, and others. Mother taught us through her poetry to have compassion for others. One poem she recited, "The Auctioneer's Gift" (S. W. Foss, 1891), was about a humorous auctioneer as he auctioned off a family's furniture while the mortgagee, who was attempting to get his money back, looked on. When we interrupted Mama to ask what was an auctioneer and a mortgagee, she patiently explained. She continued in dramatic form, imitating the auctioneer as he jokingly enticed people to bid on bureaus, beds, crockery, and a grand piano that he swore would last a thousand years.

We were, by this time, pretty judgmental of this auctioneer when he asked the audience to make a bid on a little baby's chair: "Come, come. Is all your money spent?" We could picture the "sad-faced woman who stood in silence near," breaking down and crying, "My poor baby's chair, my poor dead baby's chair!" To which the auctioneer responded, "Here, Madam. And if the owner of this chair, our friend the mortgagee, objects to this proceeding, let him send the bill to me."

Mama also taught us the importance of caring for others as she recited another standby, "Somebody's Mother," Mary Dow Brine's poem about the young boy who helped the old woman who was afraid to cross the street on a cold, wet day: "She's somebody's mother, boys, you know. For all she's aged and poor and slow." Tears still come to my eyes.

Sometimes the lessons were harsher. John Edward was a cousin, except I was too young to understand the relationship. He and his brother, J. C., spent one weekend with us. That Sunday, J. C. was outside with my brothers. John Edward, who I thought should have been out with them, was sitting up in the house like a big baby. He was as old as my brother F. D., so he belonged outside, I reasoned. I was sitting in front of the fireplace, playing with my shiny penny. I tied the penny in one corner of my handkerchief (in lieu of a purse). I am not sure if he said something that irked me or if it was just his presence. It wasn't anything fresh he did. He was just a whiner. I took my handkerchief by one end and hit him as hard as I could in the forehead with my penny. What a howl! He cried as if he were being killed. Mama stepped in, playing the heavy hand. "Give him that penny, you heifer!"

His crying stopped when I untied my handkerchief and gave him my penny. I thought of all the little packets of Kits I could have bought: eight to a package of chocolate or vanilla-flavored sweets. One penny bought at least five packets during that time. I hated John Edward and hoped he would never come to stay again.

Although I am recounting my experience of Mama caring for me as the youngest child, Mama cared for the older children from my father's first marriage as if they were her own as well. She was especially upset when Woodrow suddenly left home at age seventeen. The neighbors had not seen him; none of her inquiries brought information. It was a sad atmosphere for a long time. We didn't heard from him until one day when my mother was riding home from Columbia and spotted a young man working on a lumber truck. She came home and rushed into the living room. She was agitated and almost incoherent. It took a while to comprehend her ranting. She was crying uncontrollably. "I know it was him. It was my boy. I saw him. I saw my boy today."

None of us believed her muttering. Woodrow had been gone four years. There was no way she could have spotted him all of a sudden. She continued: "Thank God. I saw my boy today."

She was determined to go back to the spot where she saw him. She had been afraid to stop when she first saw him for fear he would run away again. Finally, Papa conceded it was worth a try. A few days later, our cousin drove Mama back to the vicinity where she saw him, and, lo and behold, they found my brother. He was now married to a young girl named Elsie. With their urging, Woodrow agreed to come for a visit the next week. Our cousin drove to pick them up. We waited in anticipation, not sure if he would come.

Woodrow kept his promise. He shared what he felt when he realized he had been found. "Had I been able to fasten the chain on the lumber when I spotted you, you would never have caught me," he said.

During the visit Woodrow told us that on the night he left, several other boys were supposed to go with him, but when he got to their house, they had changed their minds. He knew he had better not come back because it was too near dawn. I long associated Woodrow and his wife's visit with the season of the year when we gathered the pears and the grapes were in abundance on the grape vines. Papa also gathered the honey from the beehives while they were visiting.

Mama's care extended outside of the immediate family, including cousins, in-laws, the church, and community. Leading by example, she provided the lessons I would come back to throughout my life.

four

JOE ROBINSON'S LAND

In the new place, the pole house, my father expanded his business activities, running both a gristmill and a sawmill nearby. Although we were renters, we made the place ours and stayed for four years, until the visit from Henry Varn.

Unknown to my father, the land we were living on had been sold to Varn. This occurred sometime after the man who owned it died, leaving a widow. As was often the case in those days, the land was either sold or, because of debt, fell into the hands of the few with means to buy it or take it over. In this case, that was William Henry Varn. "Now, Joe, you work for me," he said as he drove up that day in 1938.

That proclamation made my father quite upset. More than just his pride as a businessman was at stake. He feared for us and our futures. As he used to say, "When you work for Henry Varn, he doesn't let your children go to school."

Varn, a banker, merchant, and large landholder in the area, expected sharecroppers' children to plant and bring in the harvest as part of the arrangement. Some families resisted and managed to get some education for their children, but they were often stuck between the need for a place to live and work and the desire to educate their children. Making sharecroppers' existence even more fragile, some landowners paid the workers with credits that could be used only in the country stores they owned, much like Varn. It was hard to break this cycle. In an interview I conducted, one of the white men who grew up in Smoaks during my time recounted how his father helped one of our neighbors go down to Varn to settle a debt, the source of which was not clear to him, to avoid losing her home. As he noted, it was well-known that some of the African Americans in the area had lost land to Varn.

Joe Robinson was not going to be manipulated by Varn and the sharecropping system. Papa was fond of saying, "I'll rule where I stay or move every day." He was strong-willed, independent, and bent on making his way in the world despite the limitations placed on a Black man. He exuded a strong sense of inner strength as well as physical strength. He had a booming, clear voice that could be heard from a distance. Relatives attributed his loud voice to his having worked around a sawmill for many years, a job that required him to talk over the noise in order to be heard.

I was too young to understand Papa's struggles. In my mother's ledger I see him trading with and working land for white neighbors who paid in a mix of cash and crops. I know enough about the harshness of segregation and race relations in the South to marvel at Papa's ability to work with Blacks and whites in the community. The ledger shows him getting paid for cutting lumber for Ernest Connor and settling other debts with him; making trades with J. D. Liston; cutting lumber for Charlie Drain ("Took"), a Black neighbor; and cutting lumber for my elementary school—and there are also the recollections of people such as Ray Thomas, a lifelong Smoaks resident who, through correspondence, shared his memory of his father doing business with mine at the pole house property: "I remember as a small boy going with my father [Joe Thomas] in horse & wagon to your father's grits mill to have corn ground into grits. The mill was pulled by what is now called a 'hit & miss' kerosene burning engine. Every so often the engine would back-fire and a large ball of fire would exit the smoke stack and would scare our horse nearly to death."

During those days I did not understand the significance of Papa's network across races and the respect people had for him; I was very young. I did get a sense of the regard with which Blacks and whites held Papa once while I was in college and went home for a visit. I took the bus from Alabama to Walterboro, where I was expecting Mama to pick me up. When she wasn't there, I waited all night in the bus station, part of the interstate Glass House restaurant chain, which typically had an adjacent Greyhound bus station. In the morning I asked the white man behind the counter if I could use the phone. I called J. D. Liston to ask him to let my mother know I was at the station. The clerk apparently overheard (or was listening in) because after I hung up, he said, "Do you mean I let Joe Robinson's daughter spend all night in the bus station?"

Papa wanted to own the land he farmed. That opportunity came in 1941 when he learned that land we were living on (where we moved after another fire earlier that year) and much land around it were for sale. Luther Thomas, a cousin of Ray Thomas's father, allowed Papa to sign the contract for 113 acres, which abutted land that Thomas also owned. Papa sought out J. D. Liston, the white neighboring farmer with whom he had a friendly relationship, and asked to borrow a dollar. Liston gave it to him, although reportedly he later said that had he known what the money was for, he would have bought the land himself. The land abutted property owned by the Listons and others whose families had owned plats going back into the nineteenth century. I do not have documentation to connect the land to any of the large plantations in the area. Even descendants of big-scale plantation owners in the vicinity where we came to own, such as the Spells, report difficulty in knowing precise locations because of the breaking up of land into numerous plats over time, but we were part of that continuing story. That clerk I spoke with in Walterboro after I sat around overnight recalled to me that morning that he remembered when my father purchased the property. (Today, when I think about it, I shrug—of course, they all would have known.)

Papa knew how to get the most from land. He and I would walk through the watermelon patch, and he would say, "This one will be ready for the Fourth of July." He would then take a small twig or piece of gravel and scratch an X on several watermelons. The year before our second home burned, in 1941, my father grew a field of watermelons that were visible from our front yard, on the other side of the highway (65, which became 61 near us) that ran through our property. What was so striking about the watermelons were the beautiful colors, which were visible from the highway. My father referred to them as Cuban Queens and Cannonballs. The Cuban Queens were long, and their colors were light green with dark-green jagged stripes. The Cannonballs were huge, round, and dark green with light-green jagged stripes. When cut open, they both had beautiful red flesh with black seeds.

Later in the year, when the season for watermelons had passed, we could walk through the cornfield and find watermelons. Occasionally, we would find a watermelon completely green in color and open it up to find yellow flesh with a taste sweeter than any we had tasted. Sometimes, when we went into the cornfield to gather watermelons, we could hear voices of others searching for our watermelons. We knew from the voices they were J. Hiers's children, but we never chased them. They lived on Mr. J. D. Liston's property, only a short distance from our field. We knew that any confrontation would result only in lies.

We had witnessed Hiers telling lies to our father before. He bought watermelons from Papa with the promise to pay for them on Friday when Mr. J. D. paid him. Friday came and passed without any word from Hiers. On Monday morning, as we were out front ready to leave for school, he came into the yard riding one brown mule with a second one hitched to the one he rode. Papa was outside with us, and we all stopped when J. Hiers rode up.

He greeted us and began, "Mr. Joe, I just stopped by to tell you the reason I didn't pay you on Friday was because Mr. J. D. paid me with a false check."

Papa chuckled. "The truck man told me on Friday that the reason he was late was because he drove to your house and he cashed your check for you."

J. Hiers changed his position on the mule, squirming, trying to decide how to respond. Finally, he got his voice. "Mr. Joe, God dammit, old man, you stay out of my business. I might pay Miss Bea, but I will never pay you." He turned the mules around and rode out of the yard, looking straight ahead. Truth was, Papa had not asked the truck man for the information; he volunteered it. The bigger truth was J. Hiers had no intention of paying Papa or Mama, and he never did.

In addition to the watermelons, we found citrons in the cornfield, long and cream in color with thick skin. We thought that their flesh was unsuitable to eat, but Mother made preserves from them.

Papa also planted fields of oats and wheat. The wheat was particularly beautiful and golden. It lost some of its beauty when it was time to use a sickle to gather the crop. Even though I was young and female, I too was required to help with the harvest. On the day when my dad took this grain to the mill and returned with flour—unbleached and bleached—we appreciated the process and were happy to see it brought to fruition. I can still recall how good it felt to walk through that wheat field.

Papa baled the hay after it was cut from a field where peanuts had grown one year. Each time Papa opened a new bale of hay, there were loads of dried peanuts. He would always lay aside a section for me. When things like this happened in my favor, it was OK to be treated like the baby of the family. When we came from school and he called, "Baby, come here," my siblings knew and would race me to the barn. They never touched the section he put aside for me, though. When he went away, he always brought back something in his pocket for me: pecans, an apple or pear, and if he had had dessert, he brought his cookies.

I was often left at home with him while the others were in the fields. I would wash dishes, and sometimes he would have me scramble eggs for him. Often an egg had two yolks and occasionally three. I was always amazed to see this. He taught me to clean, take care of baby chick cages, and sweep and clean around the outside of the cages. This was new for me, this taking care of baby chicks. The year before Papa had ordered Rhode Island Red chicks; the new ones in my charge were white, but I do not remember the breed. We kept a small light burning under their cage to keep the babies warm. It was a bad feeling to look into the cage early in the morning and find that several of the chicks had not survived the night.

But eventually most of the chicks grew up, and in particular one little white rooster. What was striking about this rooster was that he hung around the backyard. When one of us started out the back door, he, along with the larger Rhode Island Red rooster, was right behind us. They repeated the ritual when we started back to the house. They never got close enough to attack but close enough to threaten us. Papa advised, "Don't run when he starts behind you; stand your ground." "Yeah, right," I thought. "He isn't threatening to jump on you." I decided to take Papa's advice one day, but not without a switch I held downward in front of me. When the rooster got within about five feet of me, maybe less, I quickly stopped and turned while waving my switch. It scared him so much that he jumped up and fell flat. "Ha ha ha," I cackled, "now take that." I chuckled. "Even a white rooster thinks he can control colored people."

I was most pleased with myself the day Papa allowed me to curry the mule, including the tail. He taught me to talk to the mule and share with him my every movement to avoid getting kicked.

I also enjoyed combing Father's hair. He never grayed or turned bald. I used the comb by partitioning the hair, then twisting it to make curls all over his head before I combed them out. When we lived in the pole house, parents never told us about their troubles during the Depression years; I never knew we were experiencing financial difficulties. I always remember that family members visited. When my father operated the grist and rice mill, relatives came up to the house from Springtown and about and chatted while they waited.

Aunt Roxie, my mother's sister, often sent boxes of clothing from New York. She once wrote my mother about her impending arrival and instructed Mother to meet her at the old house of their father (Paa). Aunt Roxie, who cooked and cleaned for fairly affluent families in New York, still paid taxes on the property. Aunt Roxie brought three huge trunks packed as full as could be with clothes and divided them, knowing exactly what she planned for everyone. She was dressed in a light-blue satin robe, looking oh so queen-like. Once when she was coming home, she wanted Mother to meet her at Springtown United Methodist Church for camp meeting. That was one time when my father would not have been able to go. Aunt Roxie had sent him a nice suit, but he had no dress shoes. Aunt Roxie said Dad should wait at the church in the wagon until she got there. Mother persuaded him to go. He sat in sock feet, legs spread apart, anxiously awaiting Aunt Roxie's arrival. "What if she forgets?"

I knew she wouldn't. Aunt Roxie never forgot. Money and boxes continued to come to nieces and nephews in college even into a second generation. In later years, when I moved to Seattle and, on a return trip to New York, had dinner with Aunt Roxie, she presented me with a huge box of clothes. "For the babies," she said.

One muggy day, before my father took to his deathbed, I saw him coming down the road, walking unsteadily at a fast pace. He was weaving in and out and calling to me. I thought, "Now what?"

"Baby, come here." Naturally, I didn't go with joy. When I arrived, he had sat down by the side of the road. He said, "I need you to help me get to the house. My head hurts so bad."

"My head hurts just as bad as yours," I retorted.

"How do you know how bad mine hurts?" he asked.

Papa was tall, trim, and solid. However, as we made our way slowly to the house, I felt how frail his body was as he put his left arm around my shoulder and held on to me. I tried to match my steps to his. The distance was approximately five hundred feet, but it felt like a mile. This was the first time in my eleven years I had known Papa to ask for physical help from us because of illness. I was humbled and scared.

Papa died shortly after that, in November, as we prepared to bring in the harvest. After struggling to own the land he worked and rebounding from the Depression, he was unable to enjoy his earthly rewards. As my father lay dying in 1942, Madison heard him tell the pastor he was disappointed he was not able to stay with us. However, Papa left us a legacy—land—that, through our family's labor and the initiative of Henrietta, who built a home with modern features for Mama in 1957, benefited us for decades.

In the 1990s a cousin, Ben Hodges, then living in Hartford, Connecticut, not far from me, relayed how my father had sawed the lumber for him to build his house. He told me that prior to the Depression, my father owned a single and a double buggy with horses to pull them. They were outfitted with leather straps, and the buggies were enclosed. Ben recalled how when Mother drove the buggy to Springtown to teach, he and the other boys unhooked the horses and fed them while she taught school.

I was in my late sixties before I truly understood how humiliating it must have been for my father to have to sit in a wagon waiting for someone to bring him a pair of shoes.

five

MEETING THE DRAINS

I first saw them when I was three or four years old. We had moved into our new pole house. The family surname was Drain, and there were many children. They became constant in my life for years to come. We crossed the field and went through a thick wooded area to reach their house. Two younger boys in the family were nicknamed Nine and Two Pea. When I first saw them, they were wearing smock-shaped dresses made of what I think was white burlap material. I could not imagine why boys were wearing dresses and was never forward enough to ask what they wore under them. Their noses were always snotty, dripping yellowish mucus, and they sometimes wiped their noses with their sleeves. The dresses appeared none too clean. I never knew when they stopped wearing dresses and their noses stopped dripping, but one day the dresses disappeared, and their noses were dry.

A lot of activity went on around their house. In their yard were ducks, speckled-colored geese and gander, turkeys, roosters, chickens, dogs, and cats. The family also owned hogs, pigs, cows, calves, and, I believe, goats. They were also adept at hunting and fishing. Although education was not high on their list, they had good mother wit. One certainly couldn't cheat them.

On one of those long days before I started school, Mom and I were playing tic-tac-toe when four of the Drain girls came to visit. It was the first time that I knew them as Minnie, Rosena, Cora Bell, and Eliza. I was fascinated by them as they kept up the chatter. I was shocked when I heard the youngest, Eliza, say to my mother, "Miz Bea, can I have a little bit of 'bacco? See my little pipe yar?" I was surprised that someone not many years older than I was allowed to smoke. I also wondered why they were not in school, as were my siblings that day.

The shock came when Minnie told Mama that she was getting married to a man whose surname was Henderson. My mother knew the Hendersons well because the prospective groom's father and Mama's stepmother were siblings. After Mama finished congratulating Minnie and telling her about the family connection, which was too complex for my young understanding, Minnie had a request to make: "Can Baby be my flower girl?" As she asked this, she threw in the added offer to buy my dress. Somehow Mama got around to asking my opinion before she said yes to both, and I became flower girl at Minnie's wedding. Minnie moved to the Springtown/Oakman Branch area. Over the years, as the Drain children got married, they all built their homes on property adjacent to their parents and across from each other. Along that row of houses was their first-cousin Woodrow's house.

To think that the Drain children would not amount to much because school was not a high priority would be a mistake. The family did quite well. The boys were, for the most part, a handsome bunch. One of the brothers, Willie (Doc), owned a car by the time we moved out on the highway; our house burned down, and we moved back near them. He often drove us to town, appointments, and other places when needed.

A younger brother, Amos, was inducted in the army, along with my brother, Madison. Amos survived the military but died at an early age. When we were growing up, we played ball together. I was excited the day I pitched and struck him out. Our baseballs were often homemade. Our father showed us how to take a rock or corncob or any hard object, cover it with cloth, and then wrap twine or strings around it until it was the size and shape of a baseball. It worked until the strings came loose after some hard hits. We patched it up and continued to play.

It was around that time that Amos spoiled our idea of Santa Claus and Christmas. "Don't you know that is Miss Bea and Mister Joe?" he chided. With authority he pointed out, "Those pecans and peanuts are the same ones you've been seeing before." We questioned Mama, telling her what Amos had told us. She refused to give it credence.

An older brother, Charlie Sr. (also known as Took), who had a bit more of the rougher edges than his younger siblings, bought a property adjoining ours. For a while he and my mother had some conflict. One source of contention occurred when Took's hogs got out, came over, and rooted up her garden. When, yet again, she pressed Took to keep his hogs out of her fields, Took responded, "Keep your chullin home from school and let 'em chase 'em—dey ain't learnin' nootin in school nohow."

Now, that was a sock in the eye to Mama because when my father was still alive, my parents never considered keeping their children home from school to do anybody's work. In fact, Mr. J. D. Liston once approached Mom on the subject by acknowledging, "Bea, I know you don't like to keep your children home from school, but if you could just see fit to let them help me out a few days. I'm really in a jam." Mama agreed, and she and my sister worked a few days for him. I always wanted to go and be a part of the crowd. Mama let me go one day, but

Mr. J. D. asked her not to bring me another day. I was chopping up too much of his cotton. So Took was in deep water with his comment. Somehow he and Mom worked through those first touchy years and became comfortable neighbors.

Took was shrewd and sharp. When my sister and I came home from boarding school at Voorhees High School and Junior College and were hanging out on the front porch, Took came up and started talking. He commented on our weight gain. Henrietta, not one to let well enough alone, had to question him. "Well, which one of us you think is heaviest, Took?"

He had us stand up and turn around. "Now, turn slowly to the right, a bit more to the side, now turn your backs, now frontward. Well, Henrietta, I think you have Ruth by about ten pounds."

I was flabbergasted. Later I questioned, "How can he do that?"

My brother Madison reasoned that he was an astute farmer who took hogs and cattle to market. "You are in his element now."

But, as I noted, his edges were a little rough. Henrietta and I were sitting in chairs on the front porch one day in the summer, chatting about nothing in particular. We looked up and saw Took coming up the road. Took owned the property, land, and house adjoining ours, which he had bought and moved into with his wife several years after we moved there. By this time, they had been living there for close to six years. We watched his tall, rugged frame as he approached the porch.

After he exchanged pleasantries, he proceeded to say, "I jes came up here to ask if y'all got a scrub?" I decided that I would defer to my big sister, especially because I didn't understand what he asked. Neither did Henrietta. She questioned him again. He repeated, "I jes came to ask if you all have a scrub?"

"Oh, no," she answered. "We ain't got one."

Just then, my brother Madison popped out the front door. "Waah he say?" he inquired.

"Oh, shucks, Matt, we don't have one!" not wanting to answer him because she didn't understand Took.

"But waah he say?"

Took greeted Matt and explained, "I jes came to see if y'all got a scrub."

"Oooh, we don't have one."

Now Mother came out to get into the discussion. She came on the porch and greeted Took. "How are you today, Took?"

"Jes fine, Miss Bea. I jes came to see if y'all got a scrub."

"No, Took, my children don't bother to go hunting," she said, thinking that he meant a squirrel.

He looked at Mother while using all the patience that he could muster. "I mean a scrub where you scrub the floor."

We all were surprised but tried to keep a straight face as Mom said, "Oh, no, Took. We don't have one of them neither."

I should note that most of our neighbors were not as colorful as the Drains. My favorite person was Cousin Celie Simmons. We children loved her. She often sat outside the kitchen on a little porch with F. D. and me. She would take a good-size, raw sweet potato, cut it in half, and cup it in her left hand. She would then take a teaspoon and wrap her hand around the handle and scrape the potato to form bits of mushy, juicy potato in the teaspoon. The three of us took turns eating until it was depleted. I remember her as a slightly plump woman with steel-gray hair. In hindsight, perhaps she only appeared plump because of what she wore. It was the old-fashioned shape of the dress that she wore with a pocketed apron.

I do not recall whether or how we were actually cousins, but I spent a lot of time at Cousin Celie's because I was close to her daughters, Nettie (Janette), Esther, and Lillie Mae. Esther was the youngest of the three, and it was she with whom I developed a special bond, staying in contact with occasional Christmas greetings and some visits when I was in Smoaks for family affairs. Esther made my hair up in Shirley Temple curls when I appeared on stage at Field Day to tell the story, taught to me by Mother, of "The Old Woman and Her Pig," for which I won first prize. Esther also wrapped my hair for the first time. This is a process of parting one's hair into small segments and using coarse thread to begin at the root of the hair and continue wrapping it around the hair until one comes to the end. After all the work Esther did, when I tried to sleep that first night, it was too tight, and Mother had to unwrap the entire head of hair. That was my last attempt to have my hair wrapped.

Esther had a tall, wiry frame; a smooth, dark complexion; and long, black hair. Her voice was soft and low. Nettie was a bit heavier than Esther, lighter in complexion, shorter in stature, and with a voice that was a bit higher pitched. Lillie Mae, the oldest of the girls and a real joker, took fourth place in my affections for that family. Her complexion was a shade in between Nettie and Esther, and she was a bit heavier than they were.

She was also afraid to stay at home alone. For that reason, she once asked Mother if F. D. and I could come and stay with her until her other family members returned. Mother agreed. We took the long way, walking north and west up to her house. The sun was beaming hot as usual, and, as we often did, we were walking barefoot. We had also taken another of our homemade toys. We used tomato sardine cans and rigged up axles for them, placing small spools from thread, two up front and two on the back, to make wheels. Next, we attached a string to the front. We filled the oblong cans with dirt and used additional spools to represent people. Up the road we went in the hot sun. When we arrived, Lillie Mae was nowhere to be seen. We called and got no answer. We walked around the house and saw no sign of her. Our knocks and calls were answered with silence. Finally, we decided to go home. When we were way up the road, Lillie Mae came on the porch laughing it up. "Come back! I am home!" she yelled. We kept going home. When we got home and told Mama, she was just as dense as Lillie Mae. She surmised that Lillie Mae was just playing with us. She made us go back. When Lillie Mae saw us coming, she had a hilarious time. "I knew Cousin Bea would send you back!" she cackled. We vowed we would not say one word to her. F. D., a good-hearted child, was not able to stay angry, but I was not as generous.

Late one day, we learned that Cousin Celie had passed away. Sad thing was that Esther was away in school. I was too young to go to the setting up. Now we call them wakes, and they are held in funeral parlors and not at home. When my family returned home, they talked about how sad it was to see Esther rocking and singing, "Sweet home, sweet home, sweet home, happy home, my Lord. Lord I wonder if I'll ever get home." I cried for my two friends that night, Esther and Cousin Celie.

Living in proximity to families in the country meant involvement to some extent, sometimes good and sometimes not so good. Our involvement with the Drains spanned more than seven decades. On occasion the Drain girls came to help on the farm with hoeing, picking cotton, grinding cane, making syrup, killing hogs, and whatever work required help, for pay, of course. Boiling the cane juice to make syrup required a special skill, and they, along with Cousin Louise Walker, knew how to cook it just enough that the syrup was light and thin.

We had several fishponds on our farm. My family did not bother with them, but one day Rosena Drain suggested that we should muddy the ponds for fish before they dried up. The fishponds on our farm were large dugouts of earth, some circular, triangular, or oblong—the shape didn't matter. They were filled with water, sometimes as much as waist deep. Visibility was not clear. In those ponds were buckets and buckets of fish of all sizes. Some were pickerel (a long, slender, grayish fish), perch, and other fish I never knew or fail to remember.

Snakes were also swimming around in those ponds. The Drain girls knew all those snakes and could detect the danger. I knew only a rattler and hoped I never got close enough to identify one.

The technique of muddying the pond required that somebody climb into a pond with a hoe and rake in hand and begin the process of stirring up the water, raking the bottom of the pond. After my mother gave us permission, the entourage took off to the pond. The first pond had already dried up. The second pond had only a few fish. The third pond seemed just right. I feared joining the group, but I did not want to miss out on the gossip that always went on when groups got together. I joined the group, with Rosena assuring me, "It'll be all right, Baby."

I tentatively entered the water; however, all those fish, and probably snakes moving around my legs, got me climbing out onto the bank pronto! When the pond became good and muddy, a snake dashed out of the pond, right beside my feet. I nearly fainted with fear. I knew God had not put me on this Earth to stand on the bank of a fishpond to be bitten by a snake, so I decided not to tempt fate. I decided to go to the house while I had the chance. The group kept muddying the pond, and when they finished, everyone had buckets of fish to take home.

I questioned, "How does one clean these small fish?" Again, the Drain sisters had an answer. They seemed to know something about their entire environment: what was dangerous, what was safe, and how to do most things. I think they suggested scrubbing them with cornmeal to get the scales off. I kept thinking, "Not me." The fish got cleaned; I am uncertain who cleaned them. I think it was my brother, Madison. When cooked, they turned out to be a pretty good dish.

The Drain girls were there for blueberry picking, too. Magdalene Stephens, Rosena and Cora Bell, and a few other women were helping on the farm and decided we would all go blueberry picking during the noon recess hour the following day. They all showed up with their eight- and ten-quart buckets. After they had lunch and rested for a little, off we all went to the woods to pick blueberries. It was not a long distance to the woods, maybe about five hundred feet and right across the ditch. Since that day, I have not seen such huge blueberries. That section of woods was overflowing with them. I surely would not have stayed at home and missed the newest gossip. I had already missed what was discussed in the field that morning. I never got a chance to stay and hear all of it because I was always the cook. I was lucky if I spent an hour or two with the group because I always had to cook dinner. Sometimes that included gathering wood for the stove. There I was in the woods helping pick huge blueberries and having a wonderful time. It was cool in the woods, and we were protected from the boiling-hot sun.

My mother called: "Ruth, come over here! Some nice big ones are over here!" I just took off and ran to where Mother was, not taking time to look under my feet as I ran. For someone who feared snakes as much as I did, one would think I would have been more careful. Well, a rattler didn't wrap itself around my legs, but the admonishment I got from all the others kept me on full alert the remainder of the time we were there. Finally, everyone's bucket was filled to the rim, even the buckets of us who had more than one. We headed home, and the others headed back to the drudgery of the field. As for me, it was time to do the dishes, gather up wood for the night's dinner, bring in the cow, and do other chores. Believe me, the person at home always had something to do. It is one of the reasons that later in my life I hated staying at home and being a homemaker. One can work all day in the house, cleaning drawers and closets, but the people who have been out calling themselves the bread earners never pay attention to the bread cook and the cleaner.

My brothers and sisters would head north, returning to Smoaks for holiday visits, funerals, and their own burials, but the older Drain siblings never left home. Over the years when we returned home, Henrietta always made sure to stop in to visit Rosena. Needless to say, Rosena was still the sage, giving me pointers. When I was learning to drive, Madison advised me that I could not drive as fast on the country dirt roads as on paved highways. Rosena was in the car with us and gave me one last piece of advice as she chimed in: "Yes, Baby, you need to drive slow. When I was learning to drive, I drove really slowly. I drove two miles an hour." Naturally, I wondered if a car traveling at two miles an hour would move at all.

Most of the old group from my childhood have died. My brother Madison and the Drain brothers, Willie and Took, all ended up in the same hospital and nursing home before their deaths. That nursing home became the final stop for many whom I remembered from my childhood. It seemed the places to go to see everybody from home were the Colleton Nursing Home and Lovely Hill Baptist Church.

The later generations of the Drains seemed to have done well as entrepreneurs. This was evident in July 2006, when my children and I were in South Carolina for a family reunion. We decided to visit a fairly new slave museum in Walterboro. Much to my surprise, the proprietor was a Drain. Danny Drain, a grandson of Woodrow Drain, first cousin to Took and his siblings, had recently returned from New York after spending years gathering, buying, and trading African American memorabilia and slavery artifacts.[1] He had built quite a reputation in professional collecting circles, and his work was also cited by some academics. There was something about the Drains.

six

SCHOOL DAYS

In 1887 a group of Black men walked the nearly twenty-five miles from rural Smoaks to the county seat in Walterboro with a proposal for school officials. Charles Simmons Sr. had cleared and laid a plot of his own land for a schoolhouse. If he and the community built a school for local Black children, would the county pay for a teacher for the coming fall? The result was Simmons Elementary School, which was where I started my education journey and the center of my life for much of my childhood. I learned all the traditional subjects, honed my recitation skills at performances, and looked up to the inspiring adults who guided us.

Even before I began kindergarten at Simmons School, my mother was president of the Parent Teachers Association (PTA). When a program was being held at school, she always parched the peanuts for the PTA in the big oven at home. She knew how to put a huge batch of peanuts in the oven and take them out just in time for the heat to finish parching them.

Simmons was segregated, of course. South Carolina was especially aggressive passing Jim Crow laws to control Blacks and whites, and denying Blacks education was a key tactic. The state was quick to clamp down on Reconstruction reforms aimed at giving Blacks more rights, enshrining racial segregation in its 1895 Constitution. In 1896, after the US Supreme Court handed down its "separate but equal" doctrine in the infamous *Plessy v. Ferguson* case, South Carolina ruled that it was "unlawful" for different races to attend school together. In 1932 the state required segregated schools. And it didn't pay much attention to the whole "equal" thing either. A study from the 1940s found that South Carolina invested approximately $221 in facilities per white student and $45 per pupil for African American students.[1]

But the Simmons school was a monument to how, not long after slavery, Blacks set about trying to get education for themselves and their children. Esther Simmons, a classmate with whom I corresponded as I began checking my memory to write this book, shared how her grandfather gave his land for the school. Charles Simmons was the trustee, Maggie McCants was secretary,

Johnsville-Simmons Colored School. Insurance file photographs, 1935–1952.
South Carolina Department of Archives and History.

Perry Jenkins was treasurer, and Professor J. D. Garris was the first teacher. As amazed as I was by the family history Esther shared, I would learn that this was part of an underexamined chapter in African American history. The Freedmen Schools and the Rosenwald Schools, built with contributions from the former head of Sears Roebuck, have received substantial attention, but the schools that many Black communities built have not. Historian James Anderson, in reviewing the building of African American educational institutions, cites research that W. E. B. Du Bois did on the spread of these schools in South Carolina and elsewhere in the South.[2] Du Bois found that Black communities were often double taxed, for they gave land and labor to build the schools and also paid into the town coffers. Du Bois discovered that even with the Rosenwald contributions, Black communities typically provided land and labor.

During my first year, Simmons was a small, two-room school. By the time I reached first grade, Simmons and the nearby Johnsville schools were consolidated into a four-room/four-teacher school a short distance from the old Simmons school. Perry Jenkins sold the acre of land on which Johnsville-Simmons School was built to C. W. Herndon et al., Trustees Smoaks School District 5, for fifteen dollars (deed dated October 26, 1938). The property north, south, and west of the school also belonged to Perry Jenkins. (The property to the east belonged to the J. D. Connor estate, a white family with longtime roots and property in the area. The Jenkins were the second Black family I learned about who owned enough property to build a Black school.)

Johnsville-Simmons Colored School lunchroom building. Insurance file photographs, 1935–1952. South Carolina Department of Archives and History.

Many of the families who lived near the school owned their land. Others were sharecroppers. Staying in school until they finished ninth grade was impossible for some of my classmates. Most families farmed and needed all hands. It was rare that males and many females went beyond the ninth grade. My father rented the pole house property on which we lived and moved when that was sold to Henry Varn, who dictated when his workers' children could go to school. Papa found new housing not controlled by Varn; he wanted his children in school. The move meant a little longer trek to school each day, but when I was in second grade, I knew there would be school attendance from our house.

It was a five-mile walk for us, but we had no thought of turning around and going home. We were on our way to school one cold winter's morning when the ground was frozen hard from the frost. The sky was bleak, the wind was strong, and we were extremely cold. The school bus passed with the white children, some of whom we might have even played with after school or later on that week. The trees drooped from the cold; we saw no birds or other signs of life. Most of us were ill-dressed for the cold weather. We were not wearing warm boots, hats, or gloves. A few of us were wearing coats that were too thin, especially one of the boys in the group.

The next day would be the same. F. D., forever the bleeding heart, went over the ditch to try to find some kindling to build a fire. He found some grass and a few hard wood chips, and he was finally able to start a small fire. He went looking for more while everyone else squatted or stood around the small fire warming their hands. I looked at this selfish group, recognizing they were cold, but so was my brother. "F. D., don't you get another chip before you get over here and warm your hands!" I admonished. He finally did. We stomped out the smoldering fire and headed on to school, mindful that the first warning bell would soon ring.

My former Simmons classmate Thomas Warren, a retired New York City subway conductor, recalled during an oral history interview with me how we walked to school on rainy days. The oldest boys had to go out and cut wood for the potbellied stove. Once the fire was started, the room heated up, and we dried off, then it was about time to go home. I could validate that because I was one who always went to school even if it was raining. I told Thomas that I was glad that girls didn't have to help gather wood. Sometimes the school was lucky when some parents took turns and brought a wagonload of wood to school. Thomas remembered those days fondly as "some good old days." He interjected that walking those many miles to school was nothing, and we got there on time for the 9 AM start.

Johnsville-Simmons, where I attended first through ninth grade, some years before it was eventually renovated with electricity and indoor plumbing, is now a community center. But when I visited it in the late 1990s, I could still see it as it was in 1938 (see photos 4 and 5). Standing outside the building, which faced the road, I thought of how we would hoe and dig up all the grass and debris surrounding the building. There was to be no grassy lawn, just plain sand, probably to decrease the presence of snakes. On the right of the main building were two small white buildings down by the ditch: women and men privies. Each held two occupants. A surviving photo from those years is of the lunchroom, where part of the teachers' job was to fix lunches. Students in my class washed dishes after we ate while our teachers taught another grade. As the 1948 Peabody Commission documented, the lunch duties performed by teachers and students were common in the schools for Black people. It was not a practice, or a necessity, in the white schools.

In the center of the schoolyard was a flagpole. All classes and teachers circled the flagpole to recite the Pledge of Allegiance prior to the end of the school day. Those were days long before people began to openly question American claims of "liberty and justice for all." Out in the yard was also where we "wrapped the maypole" with colorful strips of crepe paper.

This was our playground, where recess was held and the scene of an all-out school fight, Simmons against Johnsville. It all began over a dark-red-colored ball about the size of a soccer ball. At recess, one student, Quillie Mae, along with a few others from Johnsville, claimed ownership for their school and refused to share with the Simmons students. When the older students heard about it, there was Hell to pay. The entire school became involved in a brawl. The principal, William J. Mason, and his three teachers were out blowing whistles and trying to restore order. Finally they did. My sister Henrietta said, "I couldn't believe I was there fighting my cousins Dorothy Lee and Octavia." They promptly made up.

Classrooms were on both ends of the main building. Up the steps to the little entranceway and through the door to the left was my second-grade classroom. The first classroom to the left housed kindergarten and first grade and was known as Miss (Semmer) Wakefield's classroom. The second classroom on the right was for the second and third grades. It was in this room that Miss (Verma) Walker taught, or ruled. More on her later.

As I entered the classroom, immediately to the left was the coatroom. The small room covered the width of the back of the classroom and had two entrances without doors. In the front of the classroom was a roll-up partition that also served as a blackboard, with chalk and crayons. On the right wall were pictures of maps and signs. One read "Support Easter Seals." This room also served as part of the auditorium. The first-grade classroom served as the second part of the auditorium and the stage. There were rows of tables and benches on both sides of a center aisle and aisles on each outer side of the benches that gave the teacher room to walk up and down them as necessary. And believe me, my teacher, Miss Walker, thought it necessary and took every opportunity to march up and down those aisles. In the far-left corner was a cabinet made of dark-brown wood with two full-length doors in which supplies were kept. It was about six feet tall. I sat at the front table to the left, my back facing the partition. My very close friends sat at the table with me. Genevieve Risher sat to my right, Justine Stephens (later McCants) to my left, with Thomas Warren and Alex Risher across from me. There was space under the tabletop for our books.

One book we used a lot was brown and rectangular, a writing manual. Pages were lined, and we used our own paper while we attempted to make the letters just as they were in the manual. Day after day, we practiced making letters. Justine, Genevieve, and I formed a habit of copying each other's cursive writing when we saw a letter one of us drew that we thought was really good. At times, it was difficult for the teacher to know which of us wrote it. Although our writing manuals were intact, other books were not. We were required to pay to rent our schoolbooks each year, but they were never new. Many of our books were discards from the white school. Often the white students' names were in them—sometimes, students we knew by name and face. Frequently, complete pages were missing, torn off, written on, or scratched through. Yet some of us, myself for example, were so happy to be in school and reading that it mattered little.

The incident I remember most about second grade was the day I sneaked my mother's book to school while she was in Washington, D.C., visiting her sister Minnie, who had been burned after a heater blew up in her home. Mother was very upset when she first got the news, crying uncontrollably at times, until she was able to leave by train to visit her. I do not recall particulars about the book, but my mother had used it when she attended Claflin Normal School. I was sharing it with my friends when my teacher saw it. She flew into a rage, snatched the book, gave me a good switching across my back, and after putting the book on the top of the six-foot cabinet, stormed out of the room. I was incensed. When she returned, I confronted her. "Miss Walker, just as you left out here, I was about to tell you I am going to get my book back."

She walked over to the corner of the room, picked up that switch, and lashed me across my back some more. "When you get tall enough to reach it, you can have it back."

I told my classmates, "If she wanted the book for herself, she should have asked for it."

With the serious outbreak of tuberculosis during the 1930s, the entire school was tested for the feared virus. When Miss Walker tested positive, there was no pity in my heart for her. My more mature self better understands how tuberculosis ravaged communities, but Miss Walker, who survived TB and returned, was not a reasonable woman.[3]

Fifty-nine years later, when I visited Justine, my classmate, to interview her for my project, she asked, oh so gently, "Ruth, did you ever get your book back?" I laughed, but it is a sore spot. I have only been in that room twice since 1946. Once was in the early 2000s, after the school had become a community center. A church group from Columbia held a service that I attended with my husband and in-laws. The room had changed considerably; the partitions that had separated the second-and-third-grade and the fourth-and-fifth-grade classrooms were removed. The stage was now at the back of the second-grade classroom, and the partition, which once served as the auditorium, was now an open space. When members of the group began to give their testimony, I so wanted to tell them about my experience. I was sitting where I had a good view of that old cabinet in my memory. It was all I could do from jumping up and yelling, "I want my book!"

William J. Mason was our principal; he also had a good relationship with my family. Mother often walked the five miles to attend PTA meetings. I stayed at school to go home with Mama after the meetings. Mr. Mason often drove us home. When we got a so-called library, books were kept in the tall wall cabinet in his classroom. I always loved checking out books—*Pilgrim's Progress* was one of my first—and sometimes he allowed me to choose two books. Mr. Mason left suddenly during the school year of 1942, marrying one of the young women of the family with whom he boarded. He returned to his home in Augusta, Georgia. We did not lose contact with him. Over the years, each time he and his family came back to visit, he stopped by to say hello. On holidays, we received cards from him with the address from "The Hill," Augusta, Georgia. He was visiting with his family shortly after I graduated from high school in 1949, and he left a gift and a card for me at church that read, "Just in case I don't get to see her." Mother knew I would want to see him, so we stopped by his in-laws, our cousins, to say hello briefly. He expressed how proud he was that I had made it through graduation. He was one person who could understand that my progress had not been a straight line from A to Z. The line had zigzagged with mud holes along the way. It had required walking across logs to cross creeks—cold, frozen, long, hot, and sandy—but as one other teacher, Professor George Curry, had observed, "The Robinson children come to school, rain, shine, sleet, or snow." (I do not know why George Curry was granted the honorific—people said "Professor" as if it were part of his name. It might have been because of his extensive education activities. He also contributed "Negro" school news to the *Press and Standard* in Walterboro.)

A new principal, Reverend Benjamin Walter McTeer, replaced Mr. Mason. I was determined to dislike him on the spot. Nobody, absolutely nobody, would replace our beloved Mr. Mason. Reverend McTeer was a tall, gangly, lanky man with huge feet on which he wore rich, soft-leathered boots that came just above the ankles. I snickered that it must have taken him forever to string them up. My mother knew the McTeer family. "They are smart—brilliant," she said. I was sure that she was mistaken, especially because shortly thereafter I would hear him perform in the role of pastor at my father's funeral. He gave a preaching rendition of the 23rd Psalm and was magnificent until he ended by saying, "And I want to say to those whom I know, Madison, Douglas, and the little girl—be strong and show thyself a man." Did that sound like someone who knew me? And suggesting that the little girl, without a name, show herself a man? Please.

But over the years, I came to understand my mother's admiration for his intellect. Some years ago I wrote a tribute to him, "A Teacher for All Times," and told the story of how he came to finish out the school year and stayed and stayed.[4] He often used his lunch hour to teach the more-complicated algebraic formulas. His favorite saying was "We learn by doing. So let's try and work it out on the blackboard." He would stay there working with a student as if he were learning it for the first time.

But don't get the impression that this man could not be pushed to the limit, good teacher, principal, and reverend that he was. I witnessed both his generosity and his anger. One day, when I was in eighth grade, I went into the classroom a little late, and he was ranting and raving. I said, "Good morning" as I hurried to my seat.

Reverend McTeer shouted, "No such thing as good morning! *Bad* morning!" as he glared at me. He was in a rage. "I will throw you up to the ceiling and catch you when you come down!"

"Wow!" I thought. "Wonder who has made him so angry?" I soon found out as he fastened his eyes on me. I could not imagine why he was so angry until he mentioned the incident of the previous day.

My classmates and I had been having a good time sitting around the potbellied stove in the classroom and ranking on the teachers. We were truly the faultfinders. My cousin Quillie Mae and I boasted we didn't have to stay at that school. We could both go to Springtown School, which was in the hometown of one of our parents. I didn't let it end there: "My mother said they are all cornfield teachers." We had a hilarious time.

To our surprise or maybe not, the teachers were in the next room, sitting around their potbellied stove, having their lunch, and listening to our conversation. Now I got it. We had been ignorant and cruel. Miss Wakefield cornered me and stated in no uncertain terms, "I never in my life waded dew to the cornfield."

When I went home and told about this exchange, my brother Madison said, "Whoa! Is that the excuse she gave? That doesn't prove nothin'. Maybe she waited until it [the dew] dried." I was lucky that angry man didn't throw me to the ceiling that morning.

Another morning, appearing disheveled and harassed, Zelma Ruth Jenkins made a quick, late rush into the classroom, hoping to be unnoticed. Reverend McTeer asked, "Zelma Ruth, how many planets are there?"

She was struggling to get into her seat after that long walk, and she looked at him with a shocked, annoyed look and asked so sweetly, "What are the planets?" It's a cliché, but one could have heard a pin drop. Reverend McTeer could only look at her with his mouth agape.

Several weeks into one school year, I had not bought my books. He questioned when I would get them, and I just left him in a huff. Later, his daughter Edythe, a fairly new teacher and Claflin graduate who taught kindergarten and first grade, asked me why I was crying. I finally told her that we had given my book money to Madison, who had left for the army. She relayed this message to her father, who was ashamed and apologetic. Madison had been one of his favorite pupils, and he was especially sad to hear Madison had gone into the army. He also knew what a huge loss it was to Mom for the oldest son to go away.

In the absence of our guest speaker, Reverend McTeer was called upon to deliver my ninth-grade commencement speech, and I was never more convinced of his brilliance. Here he was, without warning, being asked to give a speech, and he never faltered. The topic of his speech was "The Story of the Straight Pin." I can recall only parts of it. I had not heard it before and have not heard it since. It went something like this:

> The pin says, "I am so glad I am straight; it means I can stand up for my principles. I am glad that I am shiny; it means I can see a reflection of myself. It forces me to be humble. I am glad I am flexible, because it means I am not too proud to bend my back. I am glad I have a point, because it gives me a place from which to start. I am glad I am sharp; it allows me to push forward. And finally, I am glad I have a head, because it lets me know when I have gone too far and forces me to stop."

Many times in my life, as I have searched for a calm center, I have been reminded of Reverend McTeer's speech. Sitting with my former classmate Justine offered an opportunity not only to share fond memories of Reverend McTeer but also all the activities that contributed to our confidence and success later in life. Justine, who taught in South Carolina schools for many years before retiring, recalled, "They taught you how to perform before an audience and everything, you know?"

We talked about the many plays that the school performed and about Miss Barnes, a young teacher playing the piano by lamplight with someone turning the music pages for her. The memory, poise, and diction that we developed and were able to take out into the world seem to be absent in the deportment of many youths today. Two of our most outstanding performances were the musicals *Sleeping Beauty* and *Our Visit to Mother Goose Land*. In one scene I rushed in apologizing, "I am late because my new dress wasn't finished. Don't you think it's beautiful?" Now I smile and think about what a lame excuse for being late— delaying everyone else when they are all waiting to go visit Mother Goose Land! We sang the song:

> We are all excited, my, oh my
> But then, you know the reason why
> When teacher dear invited us to go
> With her to visit Mother Goose.

We continued to sing about the characters that lived on Mother Goose Isle. The excitement bubbled over when we arrived in Mother Goose Land and were met and greeted by Mother Goose, played by my classmate Annie Lee Jenkins. As she introduced all the characters, she sang:

> From Mother Goose Land, I came all the way
> To greet you dear children this glad holiday
> I am glad that you have not forgotten me quite
> And that I can be with you this glad happy night.

To this day, I see the characters and many of the students who played the parts. I see us in position on stage. Our little play, I have learned, was performed in schools around the country during those years, illustrating that much of our education and many of our experiences were similar to those of our contemporaries. Yet we were always pleased when we could relate the performances to real-life situations. I remember Thomas in one enchanting performance. When he sang the words "Last night my uncle called and said to me, 'See what I brought today?' and gently taking me upon his knee, showed me just what without delay," the students all oohed and aahed because Thomas lived with his grandmother and his uncle J. D.

Gertrude Stokes, who was not our classmate but schoolmate, sang "Nobody's Darling on Earth" by the Stanley Brothers ("I'm nobody's darling on Earth. Heaven have mercy on me"). This too was high drama because Gertrude's parents were both deceased and she lived with her brother Bossman and his family. It was also fitting because Gertrude and a schoolmate, Samuel Jenkins, were in love for that period in time. They did not marry each other, but for that moment life was beautiful. These were the times when each performance was heart-wrenching, and we made it our own Way-Beyond-Off Broadway. It showed our capacity as a school and community to care and be supportive of one another, building a foundation for our lives.

Field Days, which were held each year, gave us an opportunity to compete against African American children from other schools. I competed my first year in school, kindergarten, and won first prize for storytelling with my recitation of "The Old Woman and Her Pig." My friend Esther Simmons did my hair in Shirley Temple curls, and I felt as some stars might feel at their first movie premiere. First prize was a beautiful floral Shirley Temple dress, the first new dress I ever owned. I competed again in first grade and won my first dictionary. Years later, when I, for the first time, used the public library in Walterboro, which segregation prevented us from using in my day, I came across a report on a Field Day. A microfilm of the *Press and Standard,* dated March 30, 1939, with the headline

"Negro Field Day Friday, March 31," read: "The negro children from all parts of the county will come to Walterboro Friday to take part in a program that has been worked out by a committee appointed by the president of the colored teachers' association." The article ended with a list of merchants in Walterboro that would donate prizes to make this event a success.

The library archives also help underscore the importance that the community placed on education. In the *Press and Standard* of March 2, 1939, under a section that the white-owned newspaper labeled "Negro School News," there was an article with the headline "Colored Teachers Met at Simmons-Johnsville School." The report indicated that the group, sponsored by Mrs. Murray, our "attendance teacher" (I never knew that was her title; she was involved with teaching families canning with the use of a pressure cooker, quilt making, and nutrition), and Thelma Odom Jeans, supervisor, had met at the school the previous Tuesday. I was especially impressed to read that "a large number of parents were present." The writer, Shealey O. Davis, pointed out that "Mrs. Murray made a lasting impression on the parents as she spoke from her heart. She helped the parents to recognize more clearly that the future of their children lay in the hands of the teachers, and that they should keep them in school." Mrs. Murray's additional quoted remarks resonate with what my classmates and I took away from those school days: "We, the teachers of Colleton County, are stars of education shining in the dark night of ignorance among Negro boys and girls. Some of them are great, some are small, but each has its duty to perform." For the most part, we got it done.

seven

LOVELY HILL

The place in Smoaks that remains and will always be a part of me is Lovely Hill Missionary Baptist Church. The church was founded in 1850 during slavery. The practice in those days, if slaves were allowed to worship at all, was for them to do it under the watchful eye of the plantation owner or overseer. But as the printed church history for its 136th anniversary holds, some of the slaves wanted and asked permission from their "master" to found a church of their own. I was even more surprised that permission was granted. The meeting place was in a wooded area near the Edisto River, a temporary "brush arbor," an open pavilion with trees for the roof (common in rural areas) and not far from the current church on Highway 61.

After the end of the Civil War, according to the church's anniversary program, Lovely Hill began as the former slaves "sought a more appropriate place for worship": "The landowners in a verbal agreement gave them the use of one acre of land. They built their first church made of logs. Later, they decided their church needed a name. The women of the church declared it was such a lovely hill with rich sandy land, the church should be called 'Lovely Hill.'"

Another part of the anniversary program notes the purchase of land: "On February 14, 1911, for the sum of $5.00 and considerations, B. X. and E. R. Minus granted and released one acre to Lovely Hill Church for the purposes of religious worship ONLY. The agreement was signed and sealed in the presence of: Morgan Harrison, Mose Jenkins, Richo Jakes, Richard Walker, Charles H. Mosley, and Prestorral Jenkins, Church Trustees. The deed was recorded in the Colleton County Court on September 5, 1911."

The church was located "south by the public road known as the Charleston and Augusta highway, now highway 61." B. X. Minus, who granted the land, was a white businessman and bank director in the area. Most of the trustees were ancestors on my father's side through blood or marriage. Lovely Hill Missionary Baptist Church would become a fulcrum for faith and uplift across communities. As noted in a tribute that Congressman James E. Clyburn offered on the floor of Congress in 2009, when the statewide Lovely Hill Baptist Association, a council of churches, celebrated its first Founders Day, the first meeting of the association was in 1901 at Lovely Hill in Smoaks. I smiled when I learned this bit of history because that is the Lovely Hill I grew up knowing. Not only was it a place of worship for me, but the Reverend Samuel David Rickenbacker, whose brother and father were pastors as well, was also principal of the school I attended for tenth grade and advised Mama on my education. He and others were leaders in many ways.

It is no wonder that throughout my life it has been to Lovely Hill—now much improved cosmetically with indoor bathrooms, central heat and air, new bricks, and a new fellowship hall—to which I return to bury my loved ones, to attend family reunions, and to worship when I am in the area. As my husband and I sat listening to the choir sing on a Sunday in the 1990s, I looked upon the faces of those making beautiful music and noted that among those on the choir were classmates who graduated with me from the ninth grade in 1946 and also women and men from my childhood. I allowed my mind to wander, and a lifetime of memory invaded my senses. I look over to the left at the deacon's corner and see my father and me sitting on the long row of hard benches. This is a special memory because my father did not attend church often. I hear the minister as he tells the congregation that my father is a "big man" who owns a rice mill, a gristmill, and a lumber mill. From what I knew, even at that young age, he certainly was not bringing in big money.

The church was wooden, painted white, and had a bell and tall steeple. When I attended as a child, there were three rows of benches, with the deacons' corner to the left and the deaconesses' corner to the right. The pulpit was in the front, and the choir sat behind that. In the center of the middle aisle of the church sat a potbellied stove that provided heat in the winter. In the summer everyone used fans. Outside the entrance to the church, a stream ran across the property. It was along this stream that the two church privies were built, one for females and one for males. To the left of the church were parking areas for horse-drawn wagons and, before my time, buggies. The pump was out back, and the church cemetery was off in the woods some four hundred feet to the right. In those days the church held its baptisms a short distance away in the Edisto River. I remember clearly the day I was baptized along with my two brothers Madison and F. D. The church members sang the old baptism standard: "Take me to the waters, take me to the waters, take me to the waters, to be baptized. None but the righteous, none but the righteous, none but the righteous, shall see God. Bread of heaven, bread of heaven, feed me 'till I want no more."

As we waded out into the river, our pastor, Reverend Samuel David Rickenbacker, a stout man with a deep bass voice, performed the age-old ritual of positioning one hand behind our head and the other hand on our stomach or chest and then lowering us backward into the water. The water was biting cold, and I am convinced that the black thing I saw swimming by to my right was not a fish. We changed clothes around a makeshift tent-wagon enclosure and headed back to the church.

Madison, F. D., and I sat on the front row of the middle aisle, along with the others who were being baptized. The elders lined up and came along and shook our hands as they sang, "Everybody's gonna make you, welcome, welcome, welcome. Everybody's gonna make you welcome to that happy home." The song starts with the preacher "gonna make you welcome," then the deacons, next the deaconesses, then the members, and finally the whole church. We no longer go to the river; now the baptisms happen back behind the pulpit, where a pool for baptism is filled with water, temperature is set for the occasion, and only the church officers shake hands, but it never loses its significance for me. Some churches have added another beautiful ritual. When two of my children were baptized at Mount Zion Baptist Church in Seattle, the ceremony took place at night, and as each person was baptized and came up out of the pool, a candle was lighted by someone close. All those lighted candles with loved ones standing around the front of the church were something to behold. And when a minister says, "My sister or brother, I baptize you in the name of the Father and of the Son and of the Holy Ghost," I am reminded anew of how that belief has sustained me over the years. To this day, I consider baptism one of the most beautiful and sacred rituals in the Baptist Church.

Mama grew up Methodist. She and her family attended Springtown United Methodist Church, but when she married my father, she became a Baptist and a dedicated member of Lovely Hill. Mother always needed someone to go with her, so I was it for a while. F. D. would hitch the mule to the wagon but refused to drive to church. He was too busy working on and remaking his bicycle. Sometimes we thought it might rain, but she would say, "I am going to continue to get ready because it will stop by time to go. 'To the church the pattern gives, to show how true believers live.'" And off we would go. I also read the Bible through many times, from Genesis to Revelations, often by firelight. It was one of the few books available.

I would sometimes complain that people at church could be as vicious as anyone and that "the church is full of sinners."

Mama would say, "That's why they go to church. That's where sinners should be."

One practice that seemed odd to me was the shunning of unmarried pregnant women. We were all aware as we grew up that if a young girl became pregnant, she was turned out of the church. When she had given birth, and after she had repented sufficiently to appease the elders, she was allowed to rejoin the church, but only in the presence of the entire congregation. Perhaps that is why so few girls became pregnant as we grew up. In fact, I can recall only three young women who were placed in this position. Only one of them had been a member of Lovely Hill prior to her pregnancy; therefore, I witnessed this process just once. But even at my young age I saw something was wrong with the picture. I questioned, "Don't the young men have a hand in this baby making? So why do they not have to give an account?" Shouldn't they be judged by the same religious standards? Perhaps not, I thought. Wasn't it Jezebel the community was ready to stone and her sexual partner went free, or perhaps held one of the stones? However, I found it hard to believe that God wished it so.

Those reservations aside, Lovely Hill was a source of strength and inspiration for me. When I did interviews with classmates, Thomas Warren, who also grew up in Lovely Hill, spoke of the role models: "Cousin Otis, my second cousin, that was Aunt Rosa's son, who was a deacon at Lovely Hill, and he would always say, 'Go to school and learn all you can,' but he always said, 'Seek ye first the kingdom of heaven.'" Thomas must have been more attentive than some of us about certain things. "I used to love to hear Deacon Chisolm pray," he recalled.

It took me a while to remember he was a deacon in our church. I did not remember his prayers and told Thomas, "They must not have worn off on me because I don't remember them." But when I think about it, I realize that the eloquence and erudition of Baptist ministers such as Rickenbacker and McTeer set my standard for Baptist ministers, causing me to eschew some I would hear as I went out into the world.

Prior to her death in 1995, Henrietta installed a stained-glass window in the church vestibule with Mama's name on a gold plate, although Mama is buried in Green Pond Memorial Cemetery along with the Hodges, her family. About a decade ago, I took on a reclamation project in the Lovely Hill church cemetery. After burying my husband there in my family plot, and making room for myself, I installed a large headstone in honor of my father, who died in 1942, and his father, Peter Robinson, who died in 1931. It was a way to honor those ancestors known to be buried even if we don't know the precise location for them all. It was a way to add continuity and document their struggles, their faith, and their efforts to bring mine and subsequent generations forward. Lovely Hill is hallowed ground.

eight

THE ROOT DOCTOR

I was not yet six when I first heard about the root doctor. A couple stopped by to visit us and stayed for dinner. My sister Henrietta insisted on giving the man corn on the cob, and he kept eating it. His wife, whose hair was already gray, finally said to Henrietta, "Honey, don't give him any more. He will have a stomachache," which brought laughter to us all.

After they left, someone said, "Miss Rachel is a root doctor." I was too naive to know what a root doctor was, but my siblings were more than pleased to share their superior knowledge with me: "A root doctor is someone who can put a spell on you and can also poison you."

I expected a root doctor to look different from ordinary people. The white of their eyes would be red. They would wear layers of ill-fitting clothes with a sly look. None of these assumptions proved true. This woman, Miss Rachel Jean, was a white-haired, medium-built, grandmotherly type. Her husband, medium-framed and not very tall, maybe 5'5" or 5'6", was a dark-haired, quiet-spoken man.

But I was frightened when this new possibility was posed to me. My siblings quickly soothed me: "She didn't put any poisoning in your food tonight or put a spell on you." I was not sure how they could tell.

My mother stopped them by asserting, "She would not have put a spell on you. She does not have any reason to be upset with any of us." With that said, I didn't think about root doctors much after that. But I began to hear the term more and more as I grew up. This one and that one were identified as root doctors. Things began to happen, and I started to hear whispers of people putting spells on others.

My family became half-believers. Each year when planting season came along, our mule died. Nothing was more frightening to me than to see a mule being carted off to the woods after he died. I always thought the mule would get up and come back. I even spent time looking around the edges of the woods, hoping to spot him as he came galloping back and hoping to get a head start running into the house.

Each year as one died, Papa questioned if it could be fresh corn or some other fresh food that should not be fed to the mule. Papa never was able to discern the cause. A few years later, when we moved from the pole house onto the highway, the mules were continuing to die.

I remember the night the last of the mules became ill and died. He was a beautiful black mule. We awoke to a noise in the lot. Papa rushed out to see what was wrong. There the poor mule was staggering blindly in his stall. Papa sent for the horse doctor. I am not sure if he was a bona fide veterinarian. His diagnosis was "I am certain this is a case of poisoning." Well, that mule died, and a funny thing happened. He was the last of our mules to die. Papa bought a horse next. When he purchased the farm, Papa also bought two mules. When I left the farm, those two were alive and kicking and, as far as I know, remained so for many years.

Believing in root doctors can seem incredibly backward in 2020, but if one recalls some of the home remedies used to treat illnesses throughout parts of the country, and in some cases repackaged by Big Pharma today, there is an element of hoodoo about them. My brother Madison was prone to seizures. To treat his condition, Mama made a small pouch with asafetida, a root and herb mix, that he wore around his neck. It was called an *acifidity* or *asphidity* bag (and several other spellings and pronunciations), and folk wisdom held it would ward off the "fits."

Older people in those days seemed to have had a remedy for every ailment. Sometimes when they suspected one had worms, they administered a teaspoon of sugar and turpentine. I was still attending Johnsville-Simmons when I first saw turpentine being harvested. A hole was chopped into pine trees, and tin holders were attached to the tree below the hole while turpentine dripped in the holders. It was my first realization that turpentine came from pine trees. The smell of turpentine permeating the air was really strong as I walked to school.

Sulfur was used for many ailments, particularly itching. One drank a spoonful, rubbed it on an itchy spot, or sometimes used both methods simultaneously. Once, F. D. got into a nest of yellow jackets that attacked him on his head and stung him all over. His swollen face appeared twice its size. His entire body was affected. Sulfur was the only medication available, which Mama lavishly rubbed on his skin. He suffered the entire night until he got to the doctor the next morning.

Black Draught, an old patent medicine, was one that I dreaded. Its purpose was "to clean you out," as the old folks said. We used Watkins Red Liniment for sprains or aches, an American staple going back to the nineteenth century. I particularly liked taking the liniment for chest pains when I was around ten or eleven. My regimen was to boil water, add sugar to the reddish liniment, and sip it. I loved that sweet taste and never complained. Recently, I had the urge to know if this liniment was still being sold, so I went to the internet. Lo and behold, there was the beautiful red bottle. I read the directions, and to my chagrin the text read "for external use only."

Mama found a way to warm the bed on cold nights. Prior to putting out the fire in the fireplace at night, she heated bricks, wrapped them in an old quilt, and would say, "Hurry, push the covers back," as she proceeded to place the bricks at the foot of the bed. In later years I heard that many people suffered burns from using bricks in this manner and that it eventually caused cancer.

How am I still alive?

Much like Mama's *asphidity* bag, root doctors created special bags as amulets, working with hair, feathers, herbs, and twigs. Drawing on knowledge that slaves brought from Africa, root doctors worked to restore health and well-being, but their reputation in my day was often associated with the placing and lifting of harmful curses. Some negative incidents that occurred to our family convinced Mama that indeed people were practicing roots. When my father was ill, some visitors came. My mother swore that the reason Papa became violently ill afterward was because the woman who sat at his head had slipped something in his drink. Her accusations did not go unnoticed. The deacon came to our home to round up Mama and take her to the woman's home to apologize.

Things got stranger over time. A neighbor sent her daughter to bring my mother a quart of rice. It was not uncommon for people in the community to bring food and also to come and stay, and stay, and stay, when someone was ill for some time. My sister Mattie decided to cook some of the rice. Well, the rice turned to guck. Mama put the remainder of the jar of rice away, and what was left of the rice turned a bright red. That got Mama's attention, and it was not long before she was talking "root doctor." She began to seek their advice.

One such famous doctor was called Dr. Buzzard. Each region had its own Dr. Eagle or Dr. Crow or Dr. Buzzard. I recall my mother going to see the local Dr. Buzzard only once, combining a visit to the root doctor with a trip to the medical doctor. It was for that reason she brought me along. She wanted me to see the medical doctor because of my chest pains. He prescribed Metamucil for my chest pains. The doctor's office was in Walterboro. Dr. Buzzard's office was farther down country. I was completely taken aback when we arrived at his home. No dinky office for him. He had the most beautiful, rich home. In front of the house was a huge lake that stretched out forever. The water glistened like glass while a few blackbirds flew around and landed on the water. The lake was surrounded with a green forest, and all seemed so serene. I imagined great parties taking place there.

It was rumored that Dr. Buzzard could actually fly like a buzzard. I don't believe my Dr. Buzzard was the notorious Dr. Buzzard associated with St. Helena Island, a man who is said to have been able to control witnesses in a court case simply by chewing a potent cigar.[1] But they seem to have performed their feats around the same time.

After my father died, Mother was sometimes a believer and other times not. I recall the morning that she came into the house and exclaimed, "Well, I found out for sure." Apparently someone had told Mom to sprinkle salt around the house at an early-morning hour. Its purpose—to ward off evil spirits. It seems that as she started around the house sprinkling her salt, she bumped into a man whom we knew who was also sprinkling something around our house. He stopped suddenly and walked away.

I was a nonbeliever, but something happened years later when I was in graduate school that forced me to acknowledge my past. I was serving an internship on an adolescent ward at a psychiatric hospital. We were having a treatment-unit meeting. The psychiatrist was conducting the unit meeting; the adolescent girl who was assigned to me was having her first meeting before the entire group. She made her first mistake by asking me if I were head of this hospital. To me, this wasn't too strange. My last name was the same as the hospital director's. She erred the second time when she told the group about Dr. Buzzard and said that a lot of people believed in him. The doctors were looking very smug. I couldn't resist informing them that I came from that area of the country and that people did believe in Dr. Buzzard. Well, they all gave me a hard stare without a response. I thought my safest bet would be to shut my mouth, or they would lock me up, take my key away (all students carried a key to their offices, the elevators, and the wards), and refuse to let me go home. Whether they believed in a root doctor or not, there was, at one time in my life, a man who identified himself as Dr. Buzzard and who, it was believed, could render one helpless. And no smug psychiatrist could change that. More than half the people in that area believed in either Dr. Buzzard or a Mr. Crow. One could not diagnose them all with schizophrenia. It also confirmed my belief that in order to treat someone successfully, it is important to know the scope of their history and culture, including the role of root doctors.

During a vulnerable period in Mama's life, she made a decision that I could not fathom. This was during the time when I was still attending Johnsville-Simmons and after my father's death. She developed a relationship with a woman whom people in the community knew to be a root doctor. She, too, was an ordinary, frumpy woman, a gray-haired, grandmotherly type. Somehow she convinced Mama that some people—I never knew who they were—were after her and that she needed to move out of her house. The root doctor lived in a neat, well-kept, small house near Smoaks. She implored Mama to let her move in with us for a period until she could arrange to leave for New York. I don't think Mom took a minute to reason that if people were really after that woman, nothing would stop them from coming to our house to carry out their threat. In addition, I was concerned about what people would say about our letting the root doctor live with us. Mama gave in, and soon the woman, her slightly mentally challenged grown son, and a younger granddaughter, Mary Lee, moved in with us. She left an older granddaughter with her two children in her house. She left for New York after about four to six months, but I wondered that if she could put a spell on people, she must have put one on Mama. Nobody ever mentioned anything about her short stay to us.

Mama was scared by an incident that occurred while they lived with us. My niece and nephew, Roxie and Bubba, were visiting. At around four or five years old, Roxie was light-brown-complected with a brownish tint to her hair. One day, they were shelling peas, and Roxie found a really dark pea. She held it up between her fingers and said, "Mary Lee, this pea is black just like you." Well, Mary Lee cried and cried. Her grandmother soothed her and said, "Never you mind, child. I will take care of her before we leave." Mama swore she took care of Roxie by putting a spell on her. When Roxie grew up, began to forget, and lost some of her bright, sunny personality, Mama was sure it was because of a spell that was placed on her by the woman she brought into her home. I can't say either way. But you probably won't get me to say that root doctors don't have some kind of power.

nine

AUNT ANNA

Papa had many siblings. Among them was a younger brother, Deista, who left home at a young age. His family never saw him again. Papa told us that Uncle Deista was a gambler: "He could throw a deck of cards up to the ceiling and say stick, and they would." We were mesmerized with the tale. We surmised that our father meant Uncle Deista was good or slick with cards. As we grew up and began to read about and see other card players killing each other over a game, we began to wonder if that was what happened to Uncle Deista.

Aunt Anna was his oldest sister and the only one who lived in Smoaks. She lived near enough for us to visit—just seven or eight miles away—and she and her family became our social and emotional support. By the time I was born, two of my father's sisters had passed. One last sister, Aunt Minnie Jenkins, lived in New York City. Aunt Anna became a mother to my brother Joe Jr. after Papa's first wife died in childbirth. She said he was the size of a quart jar when she took him. Not only did Aunt Anna raise Joe Jr., but she also took in her niece and nephew Druscilla and James after their mother died.

Aunt Anna loved to sew and embroider. I was intrigued mostly with the beautiful cloth ducks she made—feet, wings, and all. There were two full-sized beds in her room, on which were thick mattresses covered with white chenille spreads decorated in the centers and with multicolored decorations on the edges. In the center of each bed was a big duck. I recall that the ducks were not completely yellow but trimmed with gingham and pastels. They sat at about eight inches long and five inches high. Aunt Anna seemed to me to be so accomplished to have mastered such an art. I vowed one day to make one for myself.

I was drawn to where Aunt Anna kept her embroidery needles and thread. The many colors of red, pink, blue, purple, lavender, and yellow were oh, so pretty! I just had to have a piece of each. I cut a length of about fourteen inches off each skein and put them in my bag to keep for myself. My bag was really a paper bag; I had no suitcase. The next day, all my pretty threads were gone. I went back to Aunt Anna's sewing box, and there were my precious threads. Well, I was not to be outdone. I took them back. The next day, they were gone again.

That aunt of mine took them back, but she left a few strands to appease me. She never said one word to me about my theft, and I did not approach her either. That was the end of my thievery at age eight or so.

I liked being at Aunt Anna's house. A blue swing hung on her front porch, and I enjoyed swinging in it to my heart's content. Aunt Anna also had rocking chairs in her living room, and sometimes, when the day's work on the farm was done, the family sat and discussed issues while they slowly rocked or maybe read the Bible before all would kneel for the nightly family prayers. Aunt Anna mostly said the prayers, long ones. I memorized her prayers, but sometimes she added some new stuff. Today I can recall large parts of her prayers. Once at our house, Aunt Anna was preparing to pray, and my sister Henrietta knelt on one knee. I looked at her as if she had lost her mind.

As I got older, O. Donald (Odonnel), Aunt Anna's son, sometimes led us in prayer. One night when we were kneeling, his young baby, Squeakie, whose real name was Naomi, got into one of the rocking chairs and had herself a grand time rocking. Her mother, Ethel, had to reach over, steady the chair, and stop the rocking. Prayers were said in the morning also, but I was never awake for those, as the farmworkers were up early.

At Aunt Anna's, I always slept with Rebecca (called Becca or Aunt Becky by her nieces, but I always called her by her adult name, Rebecca). Rebecca had a wiry frame and worked in the field; she did all the farmwork after her brothers left. The youngest of Aunt Anna's biological children, she was a real jokester. She waited until I got in bed and the lamp was out. One could now see shadows in the room. She would stretch out her right arm, bend it straight upright at the elbow, place her fingers together, curve her hand downward. "Look, Baby," she would say, using my much-hated nickname. The silhouette on the wall resembled a snake as she moved her arm in a wiggly, slow motion as if to pounce on me. I would scream with fright and hide under the cover.

I dreaded waking up in the bedroom alone. I often found myself trying desperately to wake up but had the sensation of some force holding me down in bed. Try as I might, I couldn't rid myself of the force. Folks referred to it as "a hag riding." They could be heard to say, "That ol' hag rode me all night." When I finally woke up, the room was all quiet. Not one soul was around, but I knew that hag was there watching. It was only in this house in that room that I had that experience. I would get up and make my way down to the kitchen, which was separated from the main house by a covered passageway that leveled with the house. One walked to the living room through a narrow hallway to the passageway, which led through the dining area to the kitchen. The kitchen held a stone fireplace and a slow-burning fire to take the chill out of the room. There was life there, and I felt safe. The big stove sat to the right of the fireplace with a big water tank attached on its right side. The hot water was used for dishwashing, people washing up, and other purposes as needed. There was Aunt Anna fully dressed and wearing her favorite apron with pockets. She had already made breakfast and was ready with her daily, crazy joke, which she asked and answered.

"How would you like to be the cow this morning?"

"I wouldn't like it 'cause they would pull my bags off."

I always thought, "What a silly, dumb joke," and would refuse to crack a smile.

My Aunt Anna was a good soul, though. She was in my early life and there until I left home. It was to Aunt Anna's house that my brother Joe Jr. took me the night after our house burned down earlier that day. The summer our house burned down, Aunt Anna thought I should spend some time with her until my parents got things straightened out around the makeshift housing. When she went to Walterboro, she bought two of the most beautiful pieces of fine pink fabric. She paid Aunt Laura Lee to make a dress with matching slip for me. I felt like a princess when I first wore it.

She could also push my buttons. I vacillated between liking her and wishing I had the nerve to literally choke her. Once, I think it was after Rebecca had left home, I broke a glass. Aunt Anna was so upset. "Oh, Becca will have a fit!" she said.

I had some little change, ten or fifteen cents. I took the change, gave it to her, and said, "Take this and buy Rebecca another glass. I would hate to see her have a fit over a broken glass."

I think she was so shocked that she just took the money. When I left to go home, there the money was. As with the thread, neither she nor I said a word more about it. After I grew up, I realized the glass was one of a matching set and not easy to replace.

High on the living room wall hung two portraits. One was of her husband, Morgan Harrison, and the other was of my father. I often stood on a chair to admire my father's portrait and wished I could have it. I said to Rebecca, "If you ever decide to get rid of my dad's picture, may I have it?" My father's picture is finally hanging on my wall but without its rich old frame. I took it to a family reunion to share with family members in 2006 and vowed to myself I would buy a frame that would do the portrait justice and represent that long-ago age.

Aunt Anna had grape vines that produced extra-large, marble-sized yellow grapes (back then we referred to the vines as a grape house). The vines were so strong that we could climb to the top, sit and pick grapes, or stand under the "house" and pick grapes. Once, a snake slithered across the grape vine as Rebecca and I sat picking grapes. Rebecca did not flinch, so I pretended I did not see it either. We were never permitted to pick grapes without our aunt's permission. To this day, I am not sure if Mother made the rule, or Aunt Anna, or both. One Sunday, my siblings and I walked out to her house, and no one was at home. We knew we dared not pick one grape. It was not that we were afraid of Aunt Anna. The Robinson children knew better than to pick her grapes without permission.

Late one Saturday afternoon, we received word that my sister Mattie Mae was in the hospital in Charleston. Mama knew she needed to go to her but didn't have money for the bus. She sat worrying about what to do. Finally, she, F. D., and I came up with a plan. I would go to Aunt Anna and ask Odonnel, who often drove us places and was fun to be around, to lend her the money and to meet her with it at the bus stop the following morning. However, there was a problem: it was now quite late for me to make the walk to Aunt Anna's house.

We decided I would ride the mule. Now, I was not looking forward to riding that big, tall mule. I had taken the liberty of riding him once before and had to bring him up to the porch to climb on his bare back. He tolerated me on his back all the way out to the highway, but on the way back home he stopped in his tracks, depositing me on the ground as neatly as could be. I was left leading him home. My brothers, who were with a group baling hay, thought it served me right. They wanted the mule to rest that day.

So there I was, agreeing to ride the big oaf again. My fear was that he would throw me in the deep waters that were in the road and I would have more than a swollen ankle this time. With trembling knees and my heart feeling as if it were in my mouth, I climbed into the saddle with help from F. D. I was no more than five feet tall, so I really had to stretch for my feet to reach the stirrups. I was too afraid to trot the animal because I never learned to keep from bouncing up and down and wondering if I was bouncing too far right or left. I allowed the mule to walk at his own pace for the distance, which seemed like ten miles. In a recent discussion with F. D., he said it was about three and a half miles. I cringed as we plodded through water; my hands held tightly as we entered the wooded areas where there were no houses. My inner thighs were hurting, and so was my rear end. The afternoon turned to dusk.

"Oh, Lord, what if something comes out of the woods and the mule runs? Lord, please help me!"

Finally, we came out of the woods, and I saw Aunt Anna's house. My legs were numb and barely held me up. I slid out of the saddle to the ground. I tied the mule to the fence and hobbled to the kitchen door. Thank God that Aunt Anna, Ethel, and Squeakie were at home, but Odonnel was not. One thing for sure, I was not getting back on that mule to go home in the dark.

When Odonnel came home and I explained why I was there, he did not hesitate.

"OK," he agreed. He would see Mother to the bus the next morning.

"But how did you get here?" He asked.

"I rode the mule that's tied to the fence."

"There ain't no mule out there."

"Sure it is, I rode the red mule. F. D. is going to use the black mule to bring Mother in the wagon."

"Well, he sure isn't out there now." He tried to console me by telling me the mule had probably gone home, but I knew that couldn't be true.

Aunt Anna decided she would come and stay with F. D. and me while Mother went to Charleston. So she did. She cooked, washed clothes, and took care of us while we continued going to school.

As for that big, dumb red mule, when we got to the bus stop the next morning, he was pulling the wagon.

ten

MEMORY OF A FIRE

The first time our home burned down, I was too young to recall the details, but I will never forget the second fire, which occurred in May 1941, shortly before I turned eleven years old.

At the end of the school year, different classes generally presented programs, either plays or some other form of entertainment to mark the closing of school. On this particular day my older siblings had officially finished school for the year, so they stayed at home to work on the farm and planned to come to the school's closing program that evening. My parents gave me permission to stay at my friend Justine's house until they came that night. They wanted to prevent me from having to walk five miles home, turn around and walk five miles back to school that night, and then endure another walk home. I was delighted to be allowed to go to my friend's house.

It was not long after school let out and we arrived at Justine's house, only about five minutes from school, that we saw huge black smoke clouds off to the north. The smoke clouds were extending way up into the sky and seemed to go on forever. Later, Justine's father arrived home from the same direction as the smoke was because he had been visiting his mother. He did not say what caused the smoke, and in those days children would not have approached an adult to question him about it. We continued to stay that afternoon at Justine's house and left for the school program, which began around 7:30 or 8:00.

I was excited to be at school and had just sat down to await Mother and my siblings' arrival when my half-brother, Joe Jr., said, "Ruth, what are you doing here?"

I attempted to explain to him that I had stayed at Justine's after school and that Mother and the others were to meet me here.

"Oh, don't you know? Papa's house burned down today. Mama Bea and them ain't coming."

I know I must have looked dumbfounded to realize all that smoke was coming from our house. Joe Jr. quickly said, "I'll take you home with me tonight to Mother." Joe was my half-brother, but he had never lived with us. His mother died in childbirth, and my father's sister, Aunt Anna Harrison, brought him up. So it was to Aunt Anna's house he took me that night. He woke her and her daughter Rebecca to tell them the bad news. I was too devastated, shocked, and sad to cry. Joe Jr. had been able to ascertain that no one was lost in the fire, which eased all our minds tremendously. They put me to bed as they made plans to go see my parents the next morning.

Early the next morning, Rebecca loaded the wagon with lots of things that she and Aunt Anna thought would be needed and useful for my family, and we took off. I could only sit on the wagon seat and worry about how my family had fared. We finally rode out onto the dirt highway and headed down the road. When we broke from the wooded area and saw the place where the house once stood, all that we saw was the uneven, ragged edges of the fireplace and burned ash. We pulled up into the yard, and there stood the shed, enclosed in tin. Attached to the front of the shed was a lean-to under which was a cooking stove. Aunt Anna and Rebecca got out of the wagon, and I followed. I could only hug Mama and my brothers and sisters. I don't even remember hugging my father. He was doing the manly thing, helping Rebecca with the mule and the items in the wagon.

The shed was now serving a new purpose—our home. Boards had been placed over the dirt to serve as flooring. The iron beds had been saved and were stretched out the length of the shed. We were told how my mother saw the fire, crossed the road, and made her way back to the far corner where the others were working while calling all the way. My father and brother hitched up the wagon and made haste to the house, which my father entered and began throwing out furniture. He stayed in there until the last possible moment, when others feared that the house would crash on him. He was able to save much of the furniture, including beds, the living-room furniture, pots, pans, and bedding. Other things that stood glaring in the sunlight were broken jars of fruit, vegetables, and meats that Mother had canned over the year. We learned later that the fire was a result of faulty electric wiring.

I have little or no memory of the fire that destroyed our house in 1934, but the memory of the loss of this house remains with me. We lived in the makeshift home for several months. But the fire would not be the only sad memory I associate with the shed that summer.

eleven

THE SHED

Papa was not a violent man, but a moment when his anger and, I suspect, fear overcame him has stayed with me, bringing back pain even though I was not the target. A cousin from Hell, Ellis Joseph, who actually lived in Washington, D.C., comes into the story somewhere. He was visiting in the summer of 1941, a little taller and stockier than when he'd visited several summers earlier and caused me some trouble, which I will explain later. He was truly what my father called a troublemaker. Perhaps it was just because he was a city kid accustomed to taking chances and thought it was funny.

About seven or eight of us were walking from Mr. J. D. Liston's house. His two sons, Sunny and Terry, were with us. Men were paving the Route 65 highway, which later became 61. Huge trucks and smaller dump trucks were up and down the road all day, packing rocks on the red, sandy road in preparation for pouring black tar. Some trucks passed us as they were heading home for the day. White men were riding in the cab and back of the truck. Ellis Joseph flagged one of the trucks down. It stopped quick and tight. "What are you guys doing?" Ellis asked.

"None of your damn business." The truck sped off.

When our brothers came home and told of the incident, right away it became a matter of concern for my parents. My father had already told Ellis Joseph that the men were paving the road, so he was being a smart aleck by stopping the truck. The next day he flagged down another truck. A younger man was driving. Ellis Joseph, not recognizing danger, lay down a threat: "Yesterday the other fellow driving that truck cursed at me. You tell him I don't like anyone cursing at me."

The driver only glared at Ellis Joseph as he put his truck in gear and drove away without uttering one word. Suddenly, another truck backed up swiftly, and a man in the back of the truck accused Ellis Joseph of throwing a rock and hitting him. Ellis Joseph claimed innocence as the man threatened to get out of the truck "and beat you to a pulp." We all recognized the gravity of this situation. The atmosphere was highly charged, especially because this was the same man who had told Ellis Joseph "none of your business" the day before. Had he stepped out of that truck, there would have been nothing short of a killing that day. Sunny and Terry, the two white boys walking with us, attempted to diffuse the situation by declaring one after the other that Ellis Joseph had not thrown the rock.

The man reluctantly decided to stand down and allow the truck to continue, but not before he threatened Ellis Joseph: "If I have any more trouble with you. . . ." I don't recall his exact words, but they were scary. We walked on up to our house, and none of us were in a talking mood. We knew that Ellis Joseph and perhaps others of us had just escaped with our lives, and I believe that every one of us was sure he had thrown the rock. When the truck backed up, I noticed his hand was still curled in the position that he would have used to hurl the rock. His behavior all summer had been unruly. My father felt that he was too much to deal with and a bad influence, so he sent him over the river to Reevesville to his grandparents. (I was frightened then, and today a little more afraid of what could have happened when I think of the fate of Emmett Till, visiting relatives in Mississippi a decade after the Ellis Joseph encounter out on the highway.)

I believe that Ellis Joseph's behavior greatly influenced my brother Madison that summer. He was at a very impressionable age, and he seemed impressed with Ellis Joseph. That is why my heart fell the day I saw them coming up the road—my fourteen-year-old brother coming at almost a run and our fifty-five-year-old father right behind him. We had been waiting at home for some time, and I was hoping that my father would not catch up to him, fearful of what could happen.

Earlier that day, Madison had been plowing in the field across the road. My father stood at the end of the rows directing him. "Straighten up that row. Make a wide swing here. Bring the row all the way out. Straighten up that row."

My brother finally stopped the mule, let go of the plow, and said, "God dammit, old man, you do it." He walked out of the field and headed down the road toward Springtown.

My father took off after him. To this day, I don't know if my father had him in sight as he chased him, but my brother walked five miles to my aunt Blanche's house, where my father caught up to him. Now seeing them coming back, we could not begin to guess what my father would do to him. They came in the yard, and my father said, "Wait here."

My brother waited there under the chinaberry tree with my mother and me. His eyes were big, and he knew that he had no choice but to wait. Papa went in the corn house and came out with ropes, a whip, and God knows what else. He called my brother into the shed.

We heard my brother screaming after each lick: "My mind was gone! Aaah, my mind was gone!"

I thought about trying to count the number of lashings he got, but I couldn't concentrate. I counted up to what I thought was eleven but felt too choked up to continue. We were all too afraid to intervene, but Mother said in a weak voice, "That's enough." It was not loud enough for my father to hear, but shortly afterward the beating stopped. My father then said to my brother, "Now get back out there and plow."

Later when I went in the shed, which was our makeshift home for several months after the fire, I saw that the foot of the iron bed was bent. I knew that our father had tied him up with the rope and beat him with the horsewhip, but I didn't speak about it—not to Madison, Father, Mother, or F. D. In our old age, F. D. and I talked about it to each other, but we still found it painful. Madison knew that Joe Robinson's children did not defy him, so why did he do it? Did adolescence cause him to behave that way, or was it like he said, that his mind was gone?

As I look back, I realize that Madison took the beating for three that day: for himself; for my father's younger brother Deista, who left home early never to be heard from again; and for my older brother, Woodrow, who ran away from home in the mid-1930s. My father never got a chance to bring him back and beat him. By the time we found him and he came back for his first visit, he was married. Papa's brother also ran away from him at an early age. The idea of running away was one topic he was touchy about. The year before Madison ran, my father was berating F. D. for some infraction, and F. D. chided, "Fool with me, I will run away." To which Papa replied, "Fool with me, I will cut your ass and run you away." That was the end of F. D.'s threat. Madison paid the price for all of them.

I was never sure that the relationship between Papa and Madison would not explode again because there often appeared tension between them. I felt very sure that Madison would never take another whipping from my father and that if they were to come to blows again, it would either be kill or be killed. They never reached the point where it had to be tested; my father died the following year.

Parents disciplined harshly in those days, often saying that it was better they did it now than the white man having to do it later. I received only five whippings from Papa in my nearly twelve years with him. One of them was during the time when we kids did not listen and played ball in his newly planted garden, ruining his seeds. For some whippings I do not recall specifics. The fifth could have been avoided had Papa not been so pigheaded and listened to my explanation of what really happened. Papa had an ugly habit of name-calling. He, in anger, called all of us names with the exception of my sister Henrietta. I can't recall him calling her names. I was "you big-belly sow." F. D. was "you baby-monkey-looking rascal." Mattie Mae was "you slew-foot heifer." Madison was "you flat-headed rascal."

We talk a lot today about how terrible it is for the child's self-esteem, but when I grew up, many parents thought it nothing to throw out such insults. Unfortunately, some of those child-rearing practices have continued to this day. One thing I knew was that I was not a sow and that the others of us were not heifers or rascals. I was smart-mouthed and on occasion would say, "I am not a sow." He never smacked me down when I responded. I sometimes wonder if our self-esteem was harmed and, if so, in what way. What I am certain of is that we were survivors who stayed out of jail and made a decent living for our families and our offspring, and those of us who are still alive are enjoying life's pleasures. Sometimes when I think back, I reason that it must have been difficult to be parents who were placed in life situations in which one struggled every day to earn enough to support one's family.

As for Ellis Joseph, before he turned sixteen, he was back in South Carolina again. This time he was silent, unable to try any of his shenanigans. He lay in a coffin, his mother weeping at his funeral held at the Springtown Methodist Church. Henrietta, who had stayed with his family in Washington, D.C., wept as loudly as anyone as she wailed, "Oh, Son," which he was often called. He was said to have drowned in the school's swimming pool. The telegram from his school read, "Deepest Sympathy, Principal and Faculty, Bundy School." I silently thought that he had probably irked someone and they let him drown, but I did not voice my opinion to the mourning family. Mama would have knocked me silly.

twelve

UP AND DOWN THE ROAD

When I look over the 1940 census, with the list of all the families, Black and white, who lived near what became SC 61, images from life up and down the road stream through my mind (see photo 6). We moved there in 1938 after the Adams place was sold and Varn came calling. Although we were forced to move again in 1941, after the second fire, we were not far from these same neighbors. All of the homes I lived in were part of an area the census recognized as Warren Township, an older distinction assigned to the outskirts of Smoaks that eventually disappeared.

Ernest Connor, a white man whose family had been in the area for many generations, lived in the third house from ours. He lived past Albert Hucks, a white man who lived alone next to us. J. D. Liston's house was on the opposite side of the road. Connor's house sat way back from the road at the end of a long lane. He owned property out near our school in the area called the Pineland. Among other things, he had a cow pasture and drove out in the Pineland practically each morning to take care of his cattle. Some mornings he would stop and give a few of us a ride to school. F. D. and I tried to gauge our leaving home to coincide with his schedule. That way we would not have gone too far, just far enough so that we could get a ride. Sometimes, our plan worked. Other times we had gone too far, and he would pass us with some other children already in the backseat, waving and grinning at us. No other Black schoolchildren lived past our house; only the Jenkins children lived at the opposite end of the road, and the Harrisons lived at the intersection. So it was most often either my siblings and I or some of those two families who rode with him.

Sometimes we took a shortcut through the Connor pasture. We were really frightened of his bulls and devised a plan to protect us when we used that route coming home from school. We either did not wear red or hid it (not yet knowing that bulls do not charge color). Our next plan was to run and climb a tree. We all knew how to climb a tree, but we never figured what to do if a bull stopped at the base of the tree and pawed the earth or if one of us were to fall from the tree. I, especially, should have feared falling right in front of the bull's horns. It

Page of the 1940 manuscript census showing the families,
white and Black, who lived near ours. Sixteenth Census
of the United States, Population Schedule, 1940.

was not too many years previously when I fell from the persimmon tree in our yard, causing me to stop breathing and causing my sibling to run in fear to get my mother. We figured the cattle would be on the opposite side of the pasture feeding when we got out of school, and our luck always held: a bull never chased us. Sometimes going the back way served a purpose. It was a cooler walk home on those days when the scorching sun pressed down on us. We never figured out whether it was truly a shortcut.

My best friend, Virginia, who lived up the road for several years, and I hired ourselves out to clean the Connor yard, a job that lasted all day. The yard was huge and extended all the way out to the chicken coops. Mr. Connor raised chickens, hundreds of them inside a wire fence, with special units to house them. His wife, Mrs. Ruth, and his sister always made lunch for us. One of our favorites was the ice tea they served—huge glasses with tea leaves floating in the ice with a taste of mint.

After we finished the long day of sweeping and raking leaves, we were given our pay, often fifteen cents for our very own. She also gave us a quart of lard, usually soft and runny, that we needed to be very careful with to avoid spilling most of it before we got home. There was another piece in our "pay" package, but I don't remember what. Once, for Mother's Day, we used the money we earned, and our big sisters helped us plan dinner at Virginia's house. We also asked Annie Lee and her mother's cousin, Shelly.

In my later years, as I think about our sweeping and raking, I recall the seriousness placed on sweeping yards—not just the Connors's yard but also our own—and that the goal was not just a clean and proper yard but also decreasing the number of visits from snakes who might be hiding among the grass and leaves. We didn't avoid living because of them, but they were part of the landscape requiring alertness.

From an early age I was aware that the white children rode the bus to school, sometimes riding by us as we walked. I never questioned it; it was the way things were. One day when we lived in the pole house and I was still very young, Papa sang a song of the day, his voice soft and tender, with an almost apologetic warning:

> Honey, stay on the side of your high board fence.
> Honey don't cry so loud
> You can go out and play, long as you may,
> But stay in your own back yard.
> Stay in your own back yard
> No mind what the white child do
> You can go out and play, long as you may,
> But stay in your own back yard.

I remember clearly the day he sang that song, which in the 1930s, as sung by Happy Joe Turner, even used the epithets as it tells the story of "Mammy" instructing the little "coon." It seemed to have made me acutely aware of the expectations between the races because, as I recall it, it was the same day J. D. Liston came to visit Papa and brought his little girl, Ann, and asked if she and I could play together. We played together for several years, even when we moved out to the highway. When we lived in the pole house, Mr. J. D. would come to visit with my father. He drove what appeared to be an old car that made a loud noise; one could hear him coming from far away. Sometimes he brought Ann with him. If J. D. and I were playing, it was an unspoken rule that he would disappear while I played with Ann. Papa and Mr. J. D. would sit in the car and talk sometimes for what seemed to be hours, but Mr. J. D. never entered our house. He addressed my father as Joe despite being nearly twenty years younger than my father. Papa always addressed him as Mr. J. D. When my father died, he remained in our lives, but then he sat on a big chestnut horse and carried on a conversation with my mother while she sat on the front porch or stood at the kitchen window.

My relationship with Ann soured over an incident that hurt for a long time. I had often played with her on lazy summer days, sometimes in a huge second-floor room in her grandmother's section of a huge house, which had a newer section built for her family. On this day we played with the many paper dolls and the outfits Ann owned. I was wearing a new beige straw hat, with pink, red, blue, and yellow straw intertwined. Somehow when I left her house, I forgot my new straw hat. Several days later I went back to Ann's house to get it. Ann was all apologetic, saying she didn't know what happened to it. Later, my schoolmate, who cooked meals for the family, told me that Ann's white friends came to visit her one rainy day that week and threw my hat out the window. From that day, I found excuses to not play with Ann and avoided her after I left home and came back to visit, even when Mama urged me to go over.

But I developed a lot of regard for Mr. J. D. One time after I left home and returned to visit Mom, he drove by and stopped to chat with her. She urged me, "Go over and speak to him." I pulled myself off the porch, walked over to the car, and shook his hand. "I can't tell if you are Ruth or Henrietta. I don't see as well anymore. Good to see you," he said.

I was suddenly pleased that Mother had pushed me to show some respect. After all, I had known this man since I was four years old. He had been there for my family through hard times. In later years it was he who I would see sitting on his tractor, parked by the road, giving his final respects, as Mother's funeral procession slowly made its way to the main highway.

My brother and I recently remembered him in moments from our childhood. F. D. said that Mr. J. D. would pass him driving his car and say, "Want a ride?"

"Yes, suh."

"Buy yourself a damn car then." He would then drive a bit past him, and then stop and give him a ride.

But Ann, to my way of thinking, committed an act of cruelty when she threw away my hat. I could imagine what she told her friends about that "ol' colored girl" who left her hat. She would not let on to her friends that she played with a colored girl in their absence. Yet even though I was hurt about what happened with my hat, the culture of the South would not have allowed us to play together much longer. I was approaching the age where I was required to do whatever work was needed on our farm. Ann would not be expected to do farmwork.

It was one of the many differing experiences between white and Black women. Pitching in with the farmwork, though necessary, detracted from one's sense of femininity and propriety. I was sensitive to that even as a young age and was mortified at the thought of friends seeing me in the fields. After our house burned on the highway, we moved farther back toward school. F. D., the major farmer after Madison was drafted into the army, was carrying on about needing the rows in the field flattened out. He usually did this by fastening a two-by-four board or a board of other dimensions to a singletree and fastening that to a pulley for the mule to drag. This method would flatten five or six rows at once. If someone could assist him and do that, he could use the second mule and begin the planting. This particular morning, he asked Mom if I could prepare some of the rows before I went to school. Now, I had done many things to carry my share of the workload, but I'd be damned if I was going to do that chore.

Mother thought I could do it. I flatly said, "No way!"

Mom shamed me into doing it by saying, "Well, I will try and do it."

I reluctantly agreed. It took less than a half hour for me to finish more rows than he would need. As bad luck would have it, I finished the last set just as my schoolmate and friend Aileen Hiers and her sisters came along.

I worried they would spread the word around school that I had been working in the fields, something young girls did not do.

F. D. said, "I'll unhitch the mule. Quick! Run home and clean up! Take the back way to school and go as fast as you can go. When they get to school, ready to tell, you will have beat them there." I followed F. D.'s suggestions, and I either made it to school ahead of them or entered the classroom right on their heels. Thank goodness it was a breezy morning and the sun had not begun its unbearable heat, because I think now of how sweaty and smelly I would have been.

Two other white girls in my age group who rode that school bus and with whom I played were Cornelia Ruth and Mary Evelyn. They were daughters of Clifford Risher and his brother Julius, "J. R." Cornelia Ruth had blonde hair, and Mary Evelyn was a slightly smaller brunette. For some reason, a fight broke out between the two when we were down the road from the house playing. They were hitting and pulling hair as if to fight to the finish. I stood watching them. Race relations in the South had not prepared me to know what my role was in this situation. If I tried to separate them, they could have turned on me. What if I accidentally hit one of them in the process of attempting to break up a fight? Down the road at a run came their mothers. Mrs. Sue, their grandmother, was right behind them. The mothers separated their first-cousin daughters.

Mrs. Sue pointed a long, slender finger at me and screamed, "And you stand there letting them fight!" I didn't know I was hired as a referee, and I certainly would not let on that I was at a loss as to what was expected of me.

I am formalizing "Mrs. Sue" here, but in the country, folk often slurred the word and pronounced it Miss or Miz Sue. Mrs. Sue lived with one of her other sisters, and they both wore those bonnets of the day. She also had two sons, small, short of stature, 5 foot 6 or 7 inches tall. One, Mr. Clifford, had a tendency to strut when he walked. As long as I knew the family, Mr. Clifford, his wife, and their daughter Cornelia lived with Mrs. Sue. Occasionally his brother, Julius, and his wife and three or four children visited, and stayed and stayed. Clifford Risher is listed as conducting the 1940 census along the road where we lived. He got us right, and I do note that his report recognized that Father was more than a tenant farmer. The 1940 census lists my family as Robertson; J. D. Linton is Scinton. Surely Risher knew our name; something seems lost in the translation from cursive to digital archives.

F. D. and I went to help Mrs. Sue with yard work one day. One thing that you learned when you were Black was sometimes you gave a service whether you wanted to or not. You couldn't have white folks thinking you were uppity. This, then, was the backdrop for the way my life was lived (or controlled). Yard work was one of the chores my friend and I did sometimes. It usually involved sweeping and raking the yards. As I have shared, folk in the country did not keep grassy yards. Yards were sandy with not a sprig of grass, except the yards of some whites I knew. A section of the front yard that was grassy was fenced off. Company entered from the front of the house.

That day we were ready to help with whatever work Mrs. Sue needed us to do. Up drove a couple whom we believed were the woman's daughter and son-in-law. He was driving a shiny new black car. The woman was preparing to get out of the car, but her husband continued to sit behind the steering wheel. He locked eyes on my brother and began to taunt him. "How old are you, boy?"

My brother stuck out his little chest and answered, "Twelve, sir."

"No," he jested. "How old are you?"

Again, F. D. answered, "Yes, sir. I am twelve, sir."

"Can't be," he chided.

By now, I was very concerned. The air was charged with fear. What was this man getting at? His wife was now pleading with him: "Jerry," I believe his name was, "come on in the house."

But he had to ask one more time. "Are you sure you are twelve?"

My brother was still being polite and respectful of this man. I, who was known to bristle at this kind of behavior, knew that this situation required my silence.

"Yes, sir, I am twelve."

"Can't be!" he retorted.

His wife asked of her husband, "Why do you want to know?"

He replied, "I just wonder how he got so ugly in twelve years." He then chuckled, got out of the car, and followed his wife into the house.

F. D. and I looked at each other and in unison said, "Let's go." On our way home we wondered out loud to each other what Mama might say. We had not forgotten the time when she made us go back to stay with Lillie Mae Simmons after she played that horrible trick on us, pretending she was not home. Would Mama be mad at us? Would she make us go back? When we arrived home and told Mother what had transpired, she said, "You were right to come home." I guess someone explained to Mrs. Sue what happened. She never approached us to ask why we did not stay to help her.

F. D. and I were so emotionally hurt by this encounter that we were well into our seventies before we mentioned it again. Mother had taught us that when people behave badly, it is more about what is happening with them than with you. My social work training prepared me to take it one step further. Something had occurred before the couple reached the house that day, and it played out at our expense. We had known the Risher family over the years and were amazed at what had just occurred. Although I thought that Mrs. Sue was prim and strait-laced, I never thought of the matriarch and her family as being outright rude or mean.

Mrs. Sue did come close to earning my contempt during other times in my young life. When my father was up at her house one day, she apparently told Papa about the noise that she heard from our house: "I could hear Ruth stomping her foot at Mattie Mae." I knew that I was not a gentle soul, but the idea that my stomping could vibrate like that of a giant was pretty bizarre!

Our relationship with the Rishers was mostly respectful, though. When we lived in the pole house, F. D. and I once had to walk four miles to the Risher house to deliver some difficult news. Papa had borrowed Mr. Clifford's ox to plow his fields. The ox fell down and died while plowing. Papa sent us to let Mr. Clifford know and to say that he would settle with him later. F. D. and I stopped by to look at the ox on our way to carry the news, and what we saw was an awful sight. We hadn't known that an ox was such a huge, grotesque animal.

Clifford Risher was the "rescuer" in one of our encounters with a snake. Our house had several outside buildings that were used for different purposes. Two were especially important to my world. The first was the smokehouse, which was located on the edge of the yard approximately one hundred feet from the house. The smokehouse was used to cure meats around hog-killing time. The shoulders and all other parts of the hogs were salted and then hung in the smokehouse under a small smoke fire to cure. The other shed was a huge, open building with a tin roof, approximately twenty feet in width by thirty feet in length. Underneath the shed, we stored light farm equipment.

That bright, crisp Sunday morning was shaping up to be a very warm day. Madison, F. D., and I were enjoying our outdoor playground, running, jumping, exploring, and hollering as we ran from one place to the other. We ended up in the shed with Madison, who hoisted himself, holding on to the joists as he traversed from one side of the shed, across the back and down the next side. We were watching in amazement as he did such a strenuous job of holding on, allowing his feet to dangle as he supported himself by his arms. He seldom looked up at the joists as he worked his way. Finally, he pulled himself up higher and looked up, and there to his right, almost within reaching distance, was a rattlesnake. He dropped down, and at the same time F. D. and I spotted it, too.

We raced in the house and told our father. He came out, took a look, and decided the ceiling was too tall to try to prod the snake because of its deadly leaping ability. He realized the best way was to shoot the snake off the ledge, and he sent the boys to ask Clifford Risher to please come shoot the snake. Mr. Clifford agreed to stop by on his way to church. He stopped by and shot the snake with a pistol. It fell down as we all huddled, his family and mine, afraid it would get up and chase us. When we were assured the snake was dead, we looked on, some of us farther away than others, while Mr. Clifford stretched it out to its full length. He estimated it to be between five and six feet. Pleased with himself, as I felt he should have been, he placed it in the trunk of his car to show his friends at church. As for our adventures, we had had enough for the day.

thirteen

THE GERMAN POW OCCUPATION

We were setting out bunch beans for J. D. Liston when someone ran up with the news: President Roosevelt was dead. We stopped to process and mourn the loss. I do not have great recall of world events that happened during my youth, but I remember how sad everyone was to hear that FDR had died. He was a comforting presence to us.

When the United States entered the war in 1941, I was only eleven years old, and fifteen when it ended. After my brother Matt went off to war, our days were consumed with chores even more. The war did touch my little corner of the world in some strange ways.

When the war started, we had just moved to the property we would eventually own. We were used to seeing white men working in the area, but we were frightened and speechless the first time that German prisoners of war, who were working with other white men cutting timber, came to the house asking for water. We were expected to be polite, bring glasses, and pump water for them. The whites were certainly being more courteous to them than to us. Bringing glasses never warranted a thank-you. It was as if we were the ones being occupied.

German POWs in South Carolina may seem foreign to some readers—and I had to do a little research to figure out what that experience was all about. Deann Bice Segal reports that from 1943 to 1946 the state had fourteen POW labor camps and eleven POW compounds on military installations:

> By May 1945, there were labor camps in Aiken, Bamburg, Barnwell, Bennettsville, Beaufort, Camden, Charleston, Hampton, Holy Hill, Norway, Spartanburg (Camp Croft), Witherbee, Whitmire, and York. Military installations such as Myrtle Beach, Florence, Greenwood, Columbia (Fort Jackson and Columbia Air Base), Charleston Air Force Base, Charleston POE, Shaw Field, Walterburo, and Stark General Hospital all housed POW compounds. These camps were established to ease the labor shortage in agriculture and pulpwood production in South Carolina.[1]

Although Smoaks was not included among the above-named towns, Walterboro Army Airfield (WAAF), about twenty-five miles away from us, was a military installation that had a POW compound established in 1944. Segal notes that prisoners on military installations mainly did clerical work or menial tasks; however, some were assigned to work in agriculture and the timber industries. In appendix 2 of her book, Segal provides a listing of the twenty-four compounds and installations that housed POWs along with their peak numbers. Colleton County had POWs only at WAAF, but there were other compounds outside the county that these German POWs could have come from. Additionally, Segal noted that some of these smaller camps were established to reduce transportation costs to work locations because prisoners "were supposed to be employed within thirty miles from their compound or one hour of travel time to work locations." WAAF, Bamberg, and Hampton were within thirty miles of Smoaks.

Years later I would find I was not mistaken in the view that whites guarding the POWs were certainly being more courteous to them than to us. The stateside units of the 332d Fighter Groups (the Tuskegee Airmen) were moved to Walterboro Army Airbase from Selfridge Field in Michigan because the airmen had protested the discriminatory practices at that base, but J. Todd Moye notes that the unit was met by armed white troops when its train arrived at the Walterboro base.[2] German POWs had access to facilities such as the post exchange, whereas African Americans were denied this access.

The experience with the prisoners stayed with me even though I did not understand it at the time. World events work like that when you're young. My children often ask me about what I knew of the outside world in the 1930s and 1940s. When they learned of the Shirley Temple dress I won or my efforts to curl my hair like hers, they peppered me with questions about how I would have known of Shirley Temple without movie theaters or television. I remind them that catalogs and other printed material would have carried such images. There are some things you just soak up by living in a culture. But it was only later, while researching the era to fill in blanks as I wrote this book, that I learned about some of the wilder times, such as the bank robberies that caused W. H. Varn to move his bank to nearby Ehrhardt in 1937, for better police protection.[3]

By the 1930s, northerners had taken over former plantations and visited regularly around Smoaks for the hunting and fishing they could not do during cold months back home. But there were other advantages of location that drew people to Colleton County, in particular Walterboro, the county seat. Walterboro, originally Walterborough, came about in the 1780s when planters for whom it was named sought summer homes on higher and drier land where their families could escape the malaria common to the plantations, whose locations around the river basin made them so fertile for agriculture. Walterboro became another haven in the 1920s and 1930s, prior to the full interstate. For people driving from New York for holidays in Miami, Waterboro offered a midpoint for some rest, and as Sherry Cawley's collection of postcards illustrates, the guesthouses and hotels that sprouted put that town in the middle of American dreams.[4]

Coming across a package of benne seed in a store in the Charleston airport some years ago reminded me of the horses we kept for hunters from the North. Between our house and the school was a field of beautiful golden pods growing on spindly legs, reaching half the height of an adult human. One could hear the rustle of the pods, and if they were really ripe, small seeds fell to the ground. Sometimes we caught the seeds in our hands or hats or whatever we had available. We then stuffed the seeds into our mouths or carried them home and parched them. They tasted delicious—especially when they were substituted for peanuts when making candy, for it is now sold as a snack.

Hunters planted the seeds to feed and attract the birds during bird-hunting season. The hunters rode big, beautiful, well-groomed horses. I never knew what they did with the birds after they shot them, gathered them up, placed them in the canvas bags, and rode away. I realized I did not know the type of birds the men hunted or from where the hunters traveled, but F. D. filled in the details. When I telephoned to ask him, he did not need to hesitate. "They were partridges, and they really tasted good."

"Where were the hunters from?"

"Pennsylvania. The hunters were from Pennsylvania."

The hunters were interested in boarding their horses, and Mr. J. D. approached Mama to request that she allow them to build an area to house the horses, keeping them fed and watered.

It was exciting to see those beautiful horses gazing in the enclosed pasture next to the house. They were so gentle as my brothers brought water and feed for them. The bird hunters furnished the feed. They came, saddled their horses, and rode away to hunt.

My children have all sorts of questions about the business arrangement we had with the hunters through Mr. J. D. that I cannot answer. Details aren't in Mama's ledger. I feel I am doing well enough to remember what I have. Along with the German POWs, it does show that, though tucked away from much, Smoaks was very much a part of the turmoil and shifts in lifestyle under way in the world.

fourteen

SEX AND THE COUNTRY

Growing up on a farm, I was exposed to sex and reproduction when I was four, but I didn't know what it was. One morning while home with my mother, I got up late as I usually did and wandered into the kitchen. I was drawn to the open kitchen window when I heard men outside with my father. I leaned on the windowsill and looked in the direction of the voices. I saw my father along with about seven other men. They were in the lot, a fenced-in area where a barn stood near the far back end of the fence. Horses, mules, and other farm animals were turned loose in this area and allowed to move around at will. Within the lot, in addition to the men, were two horses. I watched as the men moved around quickly, getting out of the horses' way. I saw one huge animal try to climb the back of the other. Something long and snake-like was hanging down as he tried to use his hooves and climb the back of the second animal. Both horses were moving, and the one in back kept slipping down. When he did, the long thing receded.

"Mama, come see! What is that long thing hanging from the horse?" I called out.

Well, I had never seen anyone as hard of hearing as my mother was that day. It took her forever to finally make it to the window. By the time she dragged herself to the window, the long thing had disappeared. Several times the horse repeated this act, and each time I called my mother, she came too late to see what I wanted to show her. Worse, she didn't seem to understand what I tried to describe. It was difficult for me to understand why Mother, who knew something about everything, did not know this.

As I got older, cats and dogs multiplied. Chickens hatched. I saw a cow suffering to bring a breech calf to birth. None of these were more troubling to my father than the kittens that multiplied. We must have had more than fifteen cats walking around pregnant, including some that were born maybe three months prior. Our father told my brother F. D. and me to take them in the woods. We did, only to have their mamas bring a few of them back. Finally, Papa issued an ultimatum. "Take those kittens back and don't let me see them again, or I will cut you straight up and down your back."

When my dad threatened with a whipping, he carried through. He would get his switch, a slender branch from a tree, call you to come to him, and announce his favorite saying: "I give you five minutes to get here, and half of that's gone." We knew he meant we should kill the kittens. My fear of his whipping was much worse than my fear that God would punish me. Off to the woods we went with at least six kittens. Poor scared us. We decided if we dropped the kittens on the hard ground it would kill them, but it didn't work. They were still breathing.

I said to F. D., "We gonna have to throw them down harder."

"No, I can't," he replied.

I threw my kittens down hard, one by one. I looked to my left and saw one of the mamas out of the corner of my eye. From the way she looked at me, I knew she was pleading with me not to harm her little new furry kittens.

"Lord, what am I gonna do?"

I was scared about what I had just done, but I knew F. D. had better not take his back. I grabbed his kittens, threw them down hard one by one on the little dirt road until they were all dead. This was hard, but I knew our father would skin us alive had we not done his bidding. I had already learned that when he said do it, no excuse would suffice. I also had to say a lot of prayers because I got rid of them all for both of us. We returned home not wanting to look at our father. He explained that cats could have a litter of kittens and turn around and have another litter very fast. We could not afford to have thirty cats roaming the place and, as they multiplied, keep them fed and us, too. I know it sounded harsh, but I also learned later how difficult it must have been for him to keep food on our table. I say to myself, "This was the Depression, stupid."

Along with learning about animal sexual behavior, I encountered an ugly side to human behavior. I had not yet turned five the summer that the children of Mother's sister Minnie Fox came to visit. Bertha, nicknamed Eartha Lee, and her younger brother, Ellis Joseph, nicknamed Son, came from Washington, D.C. We thought Eartha Lee was so hip, with her slender body and long legs. She could talk a mile a minute and had a smooth, clipped accent and a sultry voice. After all, she was a city girl. I really took to her. She pierced my ears, and Mother let me wear her pure-gold hoop earrings, which I lost within a month. One day, the horse was rearing up while hitched to the wagon with us in it. All the kids jumped out, leaving me in, but Eartha Lee jumped back in, grabbed me, and jumped out before the horse ran away, wagon and all. Years later, she bragged about how she saved my life. They also brought sparklers, our first time seeing them. So it was instant love for Eartha Lee. However, my experience with Ellis Joseph was not smooth at all.

Madison, Ellis Joseph, and I were playing under the pole house, which was built off the ground with enough room for us to crawl under. Once we were under the house, we could sit upright. There was plenty of headroom. It was the perfect place for shelter from the rain and sun, but also to be alone with one's thoughts. We brought all our toys—bought and homemade—under the house and spent hours in what became our family room. We were playing where it was cool, under the house that hot, muggy afternoon, when Ellis Joseph, sitting to my right, opened the fly on his pants, displaying his little red penis. He and Madison were around the same age, which was three years and eight months older than I. Pointing to his tiny penis, he said, "Baby, put your mouth down here and suck this."

My brother was sitting across from me. He looked at his cousin, his pants opened and his tiny penis exposed, and looked at me without saying a word. I was both shocked and frightened, not knowing what to say. I looked at my brother as Ellis Joseph continued to implore me. I was expecting my brother to tell him to stop, but he said nary a word. I knew we were all excited about having our cousins visit, and perhaps we didn't know what to do in the face of these special relatives from the city. Our cousins were light-complected, and his little weenie, as we called it back then, looked like a red, wrinkled worm. I had never heard of such a request before. How could I bear to do such a thing? Not getting any direction from Madison and feeling myself vulnerable, I started to ease my face toward where he was pointing. I lowered my head while stalling for time to think how I could get out of this situation when Ellis Joseph pushed my face down and peed in it. He laughed and laughed while I wiped my face as urine and tears rolled down it. Yet Madison never opened his mouth. Later that night, while I was in bed, Mother whipped me. Madison had finally gotten a voice and told her about the incident. I don't know if she whipped Ellis Joseph. I learned that I would be held accountable for anything related to my body that had to do with sex, regardless of my age.

About eight years later, I was placed in another position, and it was then that I coined the saying "Not with my body, you don't." I was walking from school that warm spring day. The only other person who was walking along was Two Pea Drain, now a big, strong teenager who wanted to express his sexuality. It was a dirt road, and I knew all the families along that stretch of road, so it had always been safe. After we passed the Simpsons off to our right, it was the last house before we turned the bend some thousand feet ahead, where we could then see

Two Pea's house. Two Pea did not always attend school, but I had never expected any violence from him. This day was different.

When he approached me saying, "Gimme some, Roos," I took it lightly.

"Are you crazy?"

He started tugging on my arm, "Come on, Roos."

The more I refused, the more determined he became. He started to pull me over the side of the road. My books fell as he pulled, and I was now using both my arms to try and dig in. He pulled me across what was once the ditch, but was now dry with pine needles, and then he pushed me back and attempted to climb onto me. I was now as angry as a hornet, but also scared. I almost gave in. Perhaps I felt I could not fight against his strength. He was much too strong. He changed his tactics and attempted to hold me down with his upper-body strength. He put his face down just near enough for me to raise my face up, clamp my teeth into his fleshy cheek, and bite until I tasted blood. He let go; I picked up my books and went the approximate mile home. I got home and described the incident to Mother.

She asked, "Did Two Pea pull up your dress?'

To which I could honestly answer, "No."

My brothers, working in the field, were whooping it up as Mother took off, walking as fast as she could to the Drain house. "It is important for his parents to know I plan to send my daughter to school, and I expect her to be safe," Mama said.

I never knew the details of what my mother said to the Drains that day. I know Two Pea never tried it again. He became a grown man with the outline of my teeth prints on his cheek. As weird as this may sound, our families did not stop associating over this incident. They were our neighbors, and we played checkers and bid whist together until I left before my sixteenth birthday to go away to school. As their children grew up and married, each built a home along the stretch of road that is now named "Drain Road," but few are left to hear the story.

fifteen

GETTING BEYOND NINTH GRADE

Ten of us walked across the stage to graduate from ninth grade at Johnsville-Simmons in May 1946. We had each copied the invitations from the blackboard onto our own paper to send to family and friends. We considered ourselves special. Staying in school until they finished ninth grade was impossible for many of the young people in our community. Families farmed, and bodies were needed to work the fields.

Even rarer was for males and many females to go beyond the ninth grade. We were keenly aware that we were, as our school motto read, "Not finished, just begun," but we had little idea of where we would go from there. None of us had made plans beyond the ninth grade. Our community did not have a school beyond the ninth grade for Blacks, and by my ninth grade, eleventh grade was required to graduate high school. Twelfth grade would become the requirement midway through my high school years. Unless they could travel the fifteen miles to towns with Black segregated high schools such as Ruffin, Black youth in my community were locked out of a high school diploma because of the systemic segregation.

On that night at graduation from ninth grade, I felt deeply that it could not end there for me. Fortunately, Mama had been working on that.

Dung the summer after graduation I stayed in Charleston with my older sister Mattie Mae but returned to find that my mother had arranged for me to attend Richard Carroll Memorial in Bamberg, South Carolina, about twenty-three miles from home. The principal was Reverend Samuel David Rickenbacker, our pastor at Lovely Hill. I roomed with Martha Rivers, her son, and her daughter-in-law. Five girls and three boys boarded there, and Reverend Rickenbacker lived next door to the Rivers.

Today, when acquaintances hear that I attended boarding school, images of elite eastern schools might first come to mind. But going away for high school was a necessity for me and my peers, a sacrifice made by families that wanted better for their children, often daughters, because the boys were needed to run the farms on which the families survived. Through a combination of family savings, relatives in the North who sent money, and jobs involving cleaning and doing other tasks, my classmates from Johnsville-Simmons and I boarded away from home to get the high school diplomas that whites could seek without worrying about tuition. I would attend a new school in a different community each of my high school years as a result of the complications of making arrangements and the money.

On a trip to conduct interviews in the late 1990s, I reminisced about the challenges with some of the classmates who had walked across that stage with me in May 1946. "By the time you finished ninth grade, you knew you wanted to do more with your life because of all those supports and somebody drumming it in your head that this is what," said Justine (Stephens) McCants, my friend from first grade who spent the five years after ninth grade at Voorhees High School and Junior College in Denmark, thirty miles from Smoaks. We were of like mind as she described some of what motivated her to see beyond Smoaks after ninth grade: "When you have to work on the farm and in that hot sun, I can tell you, I see that little red schoolhouse at the end of the road. I am not gonna do this all of my days. You married those boys from around home, that's what they gonna do, put you right in the field, back in the field. I said I'm a do better."

Just hearing Justine describe all the farmwork made me want to rub some of that itch away, reminding me of how my skin would whelp up and my lips and even my eyes would swell, almost closing when I came in contact with many of the farm chores such as picking okra, setting out sweet potato vines, spreading fertilizer, spraying cotton with a syrupy mess to kill boll weevils, and yes, picking velvet beans.

But doing better required more than just having the dream. Justine, who would earn bachelor's and master's degrees, and even start work on a doctorate during her career as a teacher, had a supportive family behind her. Although her father had died by the time she was ready to attend tenth grade, her brother Booker T, whom her father had planned to send to college but who ended up running the farm, determined that the first bale of cotton would go toward her tuition at Voorhees. As Justine, the tall, lanky one in our group, said, "I used to pick cotton 'cause I could really pick a lot of cotton 'cause I was looking toward that goal, you know, to get my money to go to school. And my father was a veteran, and I got a little aid from that. But I was a working student, too. It was hard because I wanted to be in class and to play basketball. That was my biggest disappointment. I had to go to work, and the children were going to practice basketball, and sometimes I tried to get someone to work in my place. Either I'd go early the next morning and do my chores or get someone to do my chores at the St. James Building and go to practice."

She laughed as she reminisced. But the bale of cotton was serious, the foundation for Justine's future. "They [her family] would help me get that bale of cotton, and then when it was sold, that was my tuition money. Mama would keep that tuition money."

Any change in the cotton money could undo the family plans for Justine's education. One year, as Justine shared, the cotton brought less than usual. Her Aunt Marilla knew this, but nonetheless asked to borrow the school money: "She said, 'I'll have it back by the time Justine gets ready to go to school.' Well, we loaned her the money, and up to that day when it's time for me to go, she didn't have the money. You know, finished the whole thing, no money. Here she came and opened the door and gave me some of the money. I cried so hard. But by the help of the Lord we went on."

Justine continued: "They allowed me to register without all of the money because they knew I was a working student. So she [Aunt Marilla] finally paid in little bits and pieces. She paid it back, but I told her I never, never would do that anymore when we get that bale of cotton for my school. I told Mama, 'You can't.'" Justine laughed as she told me. "I was so mad. That thing was hurtful."

"I guess," I said.

"Here I am ready to go to school and she comes, 'Oh, I don't have all the money.'"

Richard Carroll Memorial, where I attended tenth grade, was named for a Black theologian, education advocate, and community leader who was known as the Booker T. Washington of South Carolina. Born in slavery in 1860 and son of a slave master, he managed to get educated in South Carolina and North Carolina, and adopted the so-called Tuskegee model, which was focused on agricultural and vocational education for Blacks, an approach that drew funds and promotional support from white philanthropists and industrialists in the North. Similar to Washington, with whom he was friendly, Carroll argued that the path for success for African Americans was not in agitating for equality and integration, and he did not endorse the political activism and intellectually elite pursuits advocated by W. E. B. Du Bois.

Carroll, who died in 1929, the year prior to my birth, created an industrial school/home for African American youths, the Colored Fair, and other tangible, practical institutions that endured. He did this amid debates over whether Blacks should receive industrial training as opposed to more liberal-arts–oriented education, although my contemporaries had a combination of both. Today, when colleagues and friends, impressed with the intellectual virtuosity of the Northern-born and younger Du Bois, criticize the Tuskegee model, and particularly Booker T. Washington's philosophy, I remind them that Washington (and his protégés) were building schools and other resources in segregated and dangerous places full of restrictions and violence. Of course, this is the perspective of a woman in her eighties; it wasn't anything I knew about in 1946. I don't believe I even knew who Richard Carroll was when I attended the school named for him.

The state's school directory for that year lists Richard Carroll as having 119 students, with four high school teachers (more teachers and students were in the elementary school).

Martha Rivers, the woman with whom I boarded, made a special cornbread called cracklin' bread. She was the only person I knew who ever made this; she put cracklin' (pork rinds) in with corn mix and baked it. It was delicious. Henrietta, who took a break between ninth grade and more schooling, was at Voorhees, in Denmark. Headed home for the holidays, I planned to get the bus in Bamberg. Henrietta and many students had already boarded the bus in Denmark. I was so happy to see them all on the bus that I stood outside chatting with Henrietta.

"Get on the bus, girl, and talk later," she admonished me.

I did Henrietta wrong at the end of the school year of '46–'47 when we held our prom. Our scene was a forest. We strew pine branches on the floor of the gymnasium and walked over the branches while wearing our long gowns. Mine was borrowed from Henrietta, who had asked that I return it in time for her own dance. The branches tore around the hem of the gown, but I mailed it back to her without explaining in advance what had happened. She described, later, how shocked and upset she was to see her tattered gown. Julia Kennedy, the house adviser at Booker T. Washington Dormitory at Voorhees, came to the rescue and provided a gown for her.

But proms and friends aside, times were not always comfortable at Richard Carroll. I shared a bed with two other girls. I do not recall all the complications of the living arrangements, but boarding was going to be more expensive the following term. It was also the last year that one could graduate from high school after completing eleventh grade. Twelfth grade became mandatory for high school graduation. I needed to be concerned about paying for two more years of high school.

At some point it was determined that I would join Henrietta and others from home at Voorhees. Julia Kennedy did a favor for Henrietta and arranged for me to live and work at Voorhees High School and Junior College (today a four-year college). Voorhees was founded by Elizabeth Evelyn Wright, a graduate of Tuskegee Institute in Alabama. I read her book, *From Tuskegee to Voorhees,* and learned about the many troubles she had to counter to build Voorhees, which was named for a philanthropist who helped support the school. After reading her story and hearing stories my mother told me about Booker T. Washington, I knew, for me, it had to be Voorhees to Tuskegee.

One of my treasured extracurricular activities at Voorhees was joining the Elizabeth Evelyn Wright Culture Club. I owe much of what I know about social etiquette and dining manners to instruction in that club. Over the years I have met some high-bred people who did not know how to eat soup. I learned that in our club.

We sang the club song:

Club so dear club so dear, E-E-W-C, striving for things in store, striving toward one goal. There's a torch burning bright through both day and night, with one goal still in sight, lead us to the light. Club so dear, club sincere, here we'll always stand. Build for character, not for fame, and we'll be the same.

Henrietta was already a member but was in the infirmary with the flu the night that I was initiated. Somehow, I tripped while blindfolded and cut a huge gash on my knee. I was taken to the infirmary to have the gash treated because it was bleeding profusely. The infirmary was located in the lower floor of our dormitory, Booker Washington. The building was originally built in 1905 as a training hospital. Henrietta was heated up when I was brought into the infirmary, nearly jumping out of her bed and accusing her club sisters: "How could you have been so careless as to let this happen?" My new gash finally healed, but I still have the scar.

The club had an annual ball. The theme my year was "The Stardust Ball." My classmate, Ray, escorted me. He was not a boyfriend. Mrs. Kennedy drove me over to his parents' farm and asked their permission to have Ray escort me. After the cost of attending was assessed—his attire and flowers for me—they decided that they could afford it. A family member would drive him to campus for the affair. I wore a blue floor-length, lace-bodied, satin-bottomed gown, compliments of Mrs. Kennedy. When we entered the auditorium, the band was playing the song "Stardust." The room smelled fresh, and everything seemed so exciting. We entered under a blue sky made of chiffon material. Make-believe stars were attached to the material, and shining through was also a full moon. We danced, and Ray and I laughed, chatted, and acted silly while we shared a table with a slightly older couple. The man, a veteran, was from my hometown. We attended the same church. The couple was enrolled in the college department. To this day I sometimes look up at the sky and hum lyrics from "Stardust," thinking of the band playing and all those stars on that blue ceiling.

Several years later, while walking across campus at Tuskegee Institute, I saw a young man and woman sitting and chatting. The young man was one of the members of the band who played "Stardust" that magical night. Adding magic to my memories was a visit to another former schoolmate from Voorhees one August afternoon in 2005. She once mentioned that her husband had been a member of the Voorhees band. I could not remember what he looked like or which instrument he played. When she opened her door and invited us in, I immediately recognized her husband as a member of the band playing "Stardust" back in 1948. I could only smile. Such a world full of surprises.

When one entered the Booker Washington Dormitory, to the right was a huge room. A piano stood in the corner to one's left. Couches and lounging chairs were placed around the walls. That was the room where young men came calling. Some of the women were on duty to take their names and then to come upstairs and tell the girls they had a caller. This was fun but also a bit embarrassing for those of us who were younger and too self-conscious to carry on conversations in the spacious parlor.

Although the parlor was intimidating for receiving male visitors, some of us certainly found good use for it. One Saturday, Mrs. Kennedy was away, and, as always, Henrietta was in charge. There was a rule that we were not allowed to dance in that room, especially on the huge carpet that covered the floor. Some of us decided that we wanted to dance, and dance we did. One of our dormitory mates could make that piano talk. So she played "You used to be mine," *bomp-bomp*, "but look who's got you now," *bomp-bomp*, "you used to be mine, but look who's got you now," *bomp-bomp, bomp-bomp, bomp-bomp, bomp-bomp*, and we never missed a beat. Henrietta implored us to stop, but we were hearing none of it. She tried to appeal to me as her sister to respect her position, but I was having too much fun. Naturally, her only alternative was to report us. Mrs. Kennedy could hand out restrictions quicker than a cat can wink an eye; needless to say, she did just that. "No dances or movies on campus" were some of the restrictions.

A dance was on campus when I was on a restriction with a couple of other girls. We leaned out the dorm-room window and listened to the band play. The soloist was singing in a loud, clear voice that resounded across campus: "Wake up old maid, don't you know you're growing old? Wake up old maid, don't you know you're growing old? You better find you a man, if you want to keep your health." I thought right then, "You are so right, brother. If it's left up to Mrs. Kennedy, we will most definitely end up being old maids 'cause she is going to keep us from the boys for the rest of our lives."

I never had the kind of relationship with Mrs. Kennedy that Henrietta did, who had known her as Julia Childs prior to her marriage and even helped with her wedding. Henrietta was also a few days short of five years my senior. To Mrs. Kennedy, I was a hard pill to take. She told Henrietta that Leola Edwards and I were the two meanest girls to ever come from Smoaks, and she told my mother there was as much difference between Henrietta and me as day and night. One would think I would have learned to take orders, but no. Once when Henrietta was left in charge—it was her part-time job—I refused to take orders. Henrietta called in the big gun, Thelma Fields, dean of women. She came all huffy and said, "Ruth is failing to do what you tell her? Now let me buzz you, young lady. You get out there and pick up those papers around the dormitory." I got a stick, picked up about five pieces of paper, and sat down on the side steps for the rest of the day.

I was thinking about how much I detested Miss Fields and her big voice. She always wanted to buzz some young lady: "Now let me buzz you, young lady. That skirt is too short—put a frill on it." I envisioned some girl wearing a pleated skirt with a frill around the hem made to Miss Fields's specifications. Other times she was known to walk up to boys and girls dancing to slow music and announce, "Now let me buzz you [young lady or man]—we do not rock on the edge of a dime here. Move around the floor. Move around." She believed that all dances should be at a fox-trot pace: "Let me buzz you, young lady, you walking around and your hips are going woop-woop, up and down—put a girdle on." The killer was when we had the "All Women's Meetings." She would chew us out for one reason or another and then follow it up with "If you don't like it, there is the door, the door will lead you to the hall, and the hall will lead you out." Needless to say, nobody saw fit to move out of her seat.

I thought that when I left Voorhees, I had seen the last of Miss Fields, but forty-two years later, when I earned my PhD, Henrietta and my husband gave a party in my honor in Springfield Gardens, New York. Henrietta, who had kept in touch with Miss Fields, invited her to the party and asked her to speak on the occasion. Miss Fields offered me all the accolades for the hard work that I had done but could not resist referring to having to come on campus when Henrietta called her because I would not listen. She got a big belly laugh about how she restricted me.

Despite its distance from Smoaks, Voorhees was Smoaks transplanted in some ways. About five girls from Smoaks were there when I arrived. In addition, four of my Johnsville-Simmons classmates—Justine, Genevieve, Redell, her sister, Beatrice, and another from my fifth grade, Margaret Harris—lived in one of the other dormitories, Wright Hall. My friends lived on the right side of the hall in Booker Washington, and I lived on the left side, where I shared a double bed with my sister. Minnie Moye from Smoaks shared the room and slept in a single bed. We each performed a duty to supplement our keep. I did some cooking; others did laundry or cleaned the dorm. Redell, a classmate I interviewed for this project, rang the bell between classes, which helped with her tuition.

We kept our food in lockers, and from there we usually ate our lunch. I felt carefree in that I always depended on my sister to see to the lunch. One day at lunchtime, she called me aside and tried to quietly tell me we were out of food. There was one tiny end slice of bread, and she wanted me to eat it quietly without too much advertising that we were out of food. She said she would find something later for herself. I ended up eating that partial slice of bread but let her know how unhappy I was about it. Later that day when Mrs. Kennedy returned, she took Henrietta around to the corner store to open an account to buy groceries. Henrietta had a little job assisting Mrs. Kennedy and was therefore able to pay the bill.

I told this story to my daughter, Sonya, and she exclaimed, "I don't believe I am hearing this! You were too spoiled! How was Aunt Henrietta supposed to eat when you ate the last piece of bread?" As I look back over this incident, I really see how selfish I was.

We ran into other financial difficulties while at Voorhees. Booker Washington closed, forcing us to move into the renovated attic of the Wright Hall dormitory. Some of the girls at Wright Hall referred to us as "attic rats." Never one to mince words, I retorted, "Some of us are attic rats, and some, like you, are basement cats."

The move resulted in a drastic price increase to thirty dollars per month. I never realized how tight times were until I came across a letter from Aunt Minnie Jenkins, my father's sister who lived in New York, among Mama's ledger and papers. Aunt Minnie wrote:

> Dear Beatrice, In close you will fine $50.00 fifty dollars. You take this and go up and see about the girls and tell the president that you will have all of his money before school close. As soon as you get this you go and see him and let me hear from you at once
> April 6th 1948
> N.Y 26 NY 225 W 110 St. Your sister in law Minnie Jenkins
> P.S. You will hear from Roxie [my mother's sister] later but don't wait

Years later, as I read that letter, I thought of how much easier it would have been for Mother, and all the other family members who helped, if it were not for segregation and we could have ridden that bus to the high school.

sixteen

HIGH SCHOOL GRADUATE

My classmate LuLu and I walked around the circle that was in front of our dormitory. We passed the cafeteria to our right, the teachers' residence, the boys' dormitory, the administrative auditorium, the classroom building, the gymnasium, the school president's home, and the small student shop, and then we walked back to our dormitory. We tried to walk the entire campus as we reviewed the past school year at Harbison. We were pleased with our recent class presentation, under the direction of Mr. Mills, our religious educator. The twelve of us in our graduating class had represented the twelve disciples, sitting around reminiscing after Jesus's crucifixion.

As we all sat around the dark stage, I was convinced I had given the performance of my life. The auditorium was also in the dark, which lent an eerie feeling. For my presentation I said that I could never forget Jesus and all the good things he did while here on Earth. The incident I shared was that of Lazarus, who died and was brought back to life by Jesus. The strange feeling overcame me that I was back in time and witnessing this action. I thought I was that good.

Our trunks were all packed and ready to be loaded into cars to go home following the graduation ceremony that day in May 1949. We'd said our good-byes, and parents, friends, and students were waiting for us to march in the auditorium.

As we marched in, and the audience rose, I immediately saw something was not right: Mama was not there. I could barely hold back the tears. Mama had never missed an important day for me. After we marched in and took our seats, I so wanted to turn around in my seat during the ceremony to see if Mama was there, but I felt restrained from doing this. I hardly took in the ceremony. My mind wandered as I silently remembered the many times Mama had been there for me. It had not been that long ago that she had brought and left me at Harbison in Irmo, about ninety miles from Smoaks, to begin my senior year.

During the summer after junior year at Voorhees, we were unsure where I would attend school for my senior year. The remodeling and other changes at Voorhees increased costs beyond our ability to pay. Henrietta had graduated, weakening my ties to the school. Finally, Professor George Curry, the principal at Springtown, who had also started teaching at Simmons School the year before I started, came up with an idea. His home was in Columbia, the state capital, and he knew of a boarding school, Harbison, in Irmo, eleven miles away.

We seemed to have been breaking all the rules because when we arrived there, we learned that there was a prior application process. Before the day was over, I enrolled in Harbison Junior College. Its method of payment was similar to Voorhees. Students paid fifteen dollars per month and worked on campus to earn the remainder of their keep. The president of the college asked if I owned a black dress and a dark skirt. The black dress was for formal occasions, the dark skirt for chapel. Like Voorhees, Harbison required weekly chapel attendance. On Sundays we marched to chapel, and on Wednesdays boys sat on one side of the chapel and girls sat on the other side. Harbison was a bit more lenient with the separation of the sexes than Voorhees, which had different sections of the campus for boys and girls, perhaps because Harbison did not have enough space to separate us.

Harbison offered some new experiences. The school took us to Township Auditorium in Columbia to hear Marion Anderson, the world's greatest contralto. The one drawback was that we sat in the top balcony, where Blacks were segregated, whereas whites sat closer to the stage below. We saw little of what she looked like, but, ooh, that voice! It was an experience I will always remember. Sunrise Breakfast on Easter Sunday morning was also memorable. We entered the dining hall and ate breakfast by candlelight. The cafeteria was warm and aglow, simply enchanting. I was also selected president of the French Club because I had begun studying French at Voorhees. (I was in my seventies before I saw Paris for the first time, fulfilling a desire seeded in those high school days.)

None of this enrichment kept me happy, however. I started to complain about wanting to go home. Finally, one Saturday my sister came with Professor Curry, who had been principal of the first school I attended. He said that if I opted to go home, "I am not taking her in my car."

I finally agreed to stay at school but got disgruntled again. I went home one weekend by bus and sat next to a woman who was a member of the US Women's Army Corps (WAC). After hearing about her experience and seeing her in that light-brown uniform (today, the Girl Scout Brownies wear one of similar color), I arrived home with the idea that I wanted to join the WACs.

Mayfield Brown, a neighbor who visited a lot and always had an opinion to share, was there on the porch as I went on and on about how I planned to join the WACs. He jumped into the conversation, as everyone seemed free to do in those days, and stated, "Ruth, what you talking about? The only WACs you are getting is the wax in your ears." That brought levity to a tense discussion. The conversation never got beyond that day, that time, our group, and the front porch. I returned and graduated.

I was a little undone that day as high school was coming to an end. Once again, I did not have any plans beyond that May. I was also sitting there upset about not seeing Mama. I went through the entire ceremony in agony. Where was Mama? As the twelve of us got up, turned around, and started to march out of the auditorium, I saw Mama seated with Professor Curry, who had brought her. What joy and relief. The tears overflowed as they rose through my body. Of course Mama would be there.

seventeen

TUSKEGEE

I had always been on my way to Tuskegee even when I took detours.

A trip back there in September 2007 helped me reconnect with the spring-board it played for the rest of my life after graduation. The visit to campus for a convocation weekend, combined with some business meetings for alumni donors, was only my second since May 1955, when I was awarded my bachelor's degree. The first visit had been for Tuskegee's centennial celebrations in 1981, and I visited en route to a position teaching in the social work program at the University of South Florida, in Tampa, my first university teaching job after earning my doctorate in Connecticut the previous year. I drove down with another Tuskegee alumna, Norma Albright, and my daughter, Maxine, who was transferring from school in Connecticut to USF. That trip was memorable for the chance to catch up with classmates and old friends, but it did not make me feel as connected to what Tuskegee meant in my life's journey as much as the second visit.

Mother had told us of the great work of Booker T. Washington, Tuskegee's founder. At Voorhees, Elizabeth Evelyn Wright, one of the founders to whom a memorial was dedicated on campus, had written a book, *From Tuskegee to Voorhees,* and going from Voorhees to Tuskegee became my dream. But after graduating from Harbison, my only clear plan was to get to New York City. My aunt Minnie Jenkins and her daughter, Kate, visited us for vacation that summer and expressed the view that I should *not* go to New York. But I needed to go. I had to go in order to make my life complete. Finally, in October, Aunt Roxie sent for me to come to New York. I took the train to New York, arriving on October 29, 1949.

From the day Aunt Roxie met my train at Penn Station, she began to in-troduce me to a new world. She introduced me to my uncle Willie, whom I had never met, and his wife and daughter. They often came over from Mount Vernon, and Aunt Roxie would prepare a big dinner. When Aunt Roxie cooked, I am convinced she used every available pot. After she finished cooking, she used all the china, silverware, and glassware. That habit in itself was not bad. The fact that I was the official dishwasher was. It took all afternoon to wash all those dishes by hand. Aunt Roxie had done so much for my family for as long as I could remember, so washing dishes should have been a small price to pay. At least I did them without backtalking her, and my face showed no sign of disgust.

Aunt Roxie loved professional baseball and introduced me to the game. Sometimes when the Brooklyn Dodgers had a home game at Ebbets Field, she bought tickets, packed a lunch, and we, including Uncle Willie and Dorothy, would head to the ballpark. Sometimes they played a doubleheader. To be present to see the baseball greats was a wonder. We loved Roy Campanella, catcher; Jackie Robinson, second base; Gil Hodges, first base; Pee Wee Reese, shortstop; Don Newcome, pitcher, and Duke Snider, center field. When the Dodgers took the field, the roar from the crowd was earsplitting but joyous.

We were there for a game that was in the bottom of the ninth, with three balls, two strikes, two outs, two men on base, and the score 3–2 with Roy Campanella at bat. Anticipation swept through the stadium, with many of us afraid to breathe. Some years later, in the 1950s, when I was living in New York, we listened to a game on the radio. The next morning, when Aunt Minnie Jenkins took her dog Jackie out for his walk, she returned holding a card that was either white with a black border or vice versa—a mourning card. What caused us to exclaim "The nerve of them!" was what was written on the card: "We are so sorry, The Dodgers." We lamented, "Yeah, you oughta be."

The first time I arrived in New York, in 1949, looking for a job with a high school education and no job market skills, it was difficult to find work that paid a reasonable salary. A brief stint working in a laundromat did not augur a satisfying future. It didn't take me long to see that in New York a high school diploma would not move me toward a comfortable, fulfilling life.

Aunt Minnie asked, "What was your original goal?"

"I wanted to go to Tuskegee."

"Do you still want to go?"

When I answered "Yes," her response was "Then you have to make it happen."

I got the Tuskegee catalog, completed my application, and was accepted. Aunt Minnie mailed my first tuition payment. As I made the long train ride to Tuskegee, I was not sure what to expect, nor did I know how I would finance my education. There would be many hurdles along the way, emotional, financial, physical, and social, but to come away with that degree in hand would be the beginning of dreams being realized. Years later, when I applied for jobs, graduate school, or whatever else I became interested in and was asked, "What makes you think you can do this?" I was tempted to answer, "If only you could walk a mile in my shoes."

From Tuskegee alumna to PhD, the highest
education achievement. Photo by Sevim Yolacti.

The trip to campus in 2007 helped me connect with a part of the journey that made so much else possible. As a returning alumna, I was invited to don regalia and join the line of faculty as they marched into chapel Sunday morning. What a delight. I gathered my doctoral robe with its distinctive markings from the University of Connecticut, but somehow between packing and traveling to the airport, we realized that I had left my precious robe behind. While waiting to board the plane, we managed to get in touch with someone in the president's office, who promised to have a robe waiting. It was there when my three adult children and I arrived in Tuskegee, after a flight from Hartford to Atlanta and then Montgomery, where we picked up a car for the ride to campus (see photo 7).

Maybe the last-minute scramble for the robe was a fitting nod to history. One of my first chores when I arrived at Tuskegee all those years ago was to go to the campus seamstress, pay forty dollars, and be fitted for a navy-blue skirt, two long-sleeve white blouses, a full cape, and a bow tie, which we wore along with black oxford shoes on our march to chapel on Sunday mornings.

In 2007, as faculty and eminent "presidential associates" (donors) prepared to march into chapel, I questioned one of the professors, "What, no students in capes?" I didn't know whether to mourn the loss or rejoice. I used to think we were special when we formed that single-file "line of march" to chapel each week. Of course, there was no cutting chapel because the roll was taken right there in line, and Miss Peters was there to assure that no one left line and returned to the dormitory. Leaving would not have worked because house advisers were in each dorm and there was only the front door waiting for some student

"Line of march" to chapel at Tuskegee Institute, ca. 1950. Students in military training led the line of march. Courtesy of Tuskegee University Archives.

to break the rule. The march to chapel was built on tradition, and members of the community stood on the side of the streets as the "line of march" passed. One year when the millionaires made a visit to campus—Rockefeller and others of his good fortune—we had to march to chapel, and it was not even a Sunday, but a Saturday instead. Naturally, I voiced my dislike for having to march. Miss Peters stared me down and told some tale about MacArthur and how he got into trouble with his mouth. Naturally, I was not going to let her get by with that, so I said, "I still don't want to march." I got another dangerous stare, so I stopped while I was ahead (see photo 8).

The practice of men sitting on one side of the chapel and women on the other had ended long before my 2007 visit. I was struck by how young the students were. I could not have imagined ever being that young. No uniforms, and men and women students sitting all together. I wondered, "Where is my old Tuskegee?" But then the choir rose and sang:

> King Jesus is a'listening all day long
> King Jesus is a'listening all day long
> King Jesus is a'listening all day long
> To hear some sinner pray.

The spiritual is signature Tuskegee choir, which became internationally famous as it gave concerts at Radio City Music Hall and toured the country. It recorded

Tuskegee Chapel, ca. 1906. Designed by Robert R. Taylor, who was the
first African American graduate of the Massachusetts Institute of
Technology. The chapel, with its famous singing stained-glass windows,
burned in 1957. A replacement was built on the same site. Detroit Publishing
Company. Library of Congress, Prints and Photographs Division.

a highly regarded album in 1954, conducted by William Levi Dawson, a prolific
composer and one of the campus luminaries. When I heard the choir, I knew I
was home at Tuskegee, there to pay homage (see photo 9).

We stayed in a conference center where there had been a guesthouse at
which I had worked part-time as a student to help defray the cost of my college
expenses. It felt good to stand in the building and share with my children the
experience of how lean those years were as I struggled through college. I was
able to show them the different dormitories I lived in, starting with James Hall,
which was then being renovated. I shared the room with two sisters from Tampa
my first quarter there. After one sister left, homesick, another young girl from
Florida, Lillie Miller, became our roommate. Our room was right on the corner
as one turned the curve coming down from the Nurses Home and diagonally
across from the John Jay Hospital.

I showed them where our boyfriends and other friends came to the window to chitchat. Sometimes we held serious discussions. Once, I developed a bad cough, and the house adviser, Miss Hannah, came to my room and insisted on taking me to the hospital, but not before she let me know that she was sure I had caught cold by talking to boys from that window. Ha! And we thought we were being so slick.

I lived at Douglass Hall with Laura Porch Pullman ("Rooms," an affectionate term that we used for our roommates or their boyfriends). My children are aware of Laura because she and I maintain a relationship. I told them about the barracks we lived in for one school year, which are no longer there, replaced by any number of newly constructed buildings. When I showed them Tompkins Hall, where all students were required to eat meals, pointing out its distance from some of the dormitories, my youngest daughter commented, "I would had to have starved rather than walk that far." Tompkins Hall was our cafeteria, but it also housed students' recreation space along with a snack counter. I teased that I was so good at bid whist, I could have majored in "recology."

As a student I had been aware of the accomplishments of George Washington Carver, whom Booker T. Washington personally brought to Tuskegee to teach and research, but I had not grasped the depth of Carver's research until my family and I toured the George Washington Carver Museum on campus. A former slave who became a preeminent agricultural scientist, Carver accomplished far more than the bits of information about peanut butter that are rationed to the public during Black History Month. He invented hundreds of products, including cosmetics, foods, and textiles, using peanuts, sweet potatoes, and soybeans from the Alabama soil; introduced cotton-peanut crop rotation; and with his pioneering Jesup Wagon went out into the community to provide agricultural training to former slaves who were sharecropping. Perhaps seeing the artifacts and photos with my children, and the fact that I had the time to take in things without the problems of daily living I experienced as a student, allowed me to open my mind and eyes to the wonders of Carver. A film about Booker T. Washington and George Washington Carver relayed how Carver lived Washington's philosophy of learning by doing. At Tuskegee, Washington, students, and faculty made the bricks and stones that built up the campus, including Washington's Victorian-style home, a historically designated landmark, and twenty-two other buildings. Those distinctive bricks have made Tuskegee a prominent masonry center as well. Over and over that weekend, I heard the Booker T. Washington saying "We learn by doing." I wondered how I could have missed the impact of the phrase when I was a student. How did I fail to connect it to Johnsville-Simmons grade school

Tuskeana Yearbook, 1955 (Tuskegee Institute).
My senior-year photograph is on the bottom left.

and Reverend Walter McTeer sending us to the blackboard and saying "We learn by doing"?

It was not that I went through Tuskegee failing to appreciate its importance and some of our privilege as part of its legacy, my struggles aside. During my time as a student, Thurgood Marshall, fresh from his *Brown vs. Board of Education* win at the Supreme Court, visited, as did alumnus Ralph Ellison and tennis great Althea Gibson. On the faculty, there were giants, although some of their greatness was more fully realized in the 1960s, and I would learn of their accomplishments as I attended conferences or was engaged in other activities in later life (see photo 10).

Charles Gomillion, dean of students, was one such person. When Alabama realigned voting lines and placed most Blacks outside of the Tuskegee city voting districts, Gomillion brought a lawsuit that eventually led to a US Supreme Court case, *Gomillion v. Lightfoot,* that was decided in his favor and became a standard-bearer for subsequent gerrymandering cases.[1] That lawsuit was among many of his civil rights initiatives over the years, although my most immediate appreciation for Gomillion came during a moment of personal crisis. My mother was rarely able to contribute money for my tuition. She had managed to free up some to send to me but was swindled of it right before tuition was due. When I went in to pay my tuition, I was $100 short. I went to the loan office looking for help but was harshly rejected. I was almost in tears as I left that office. What I did not know was that Dean Gomillion's office door was open and he had been listening to my encounter. He called me into his office. "How much do you need?" he asked.

When I told him, he reached into his desk, pulled out his checkbook, and wrote a check for $100. I never forgot that. On my trip in 2007, when one of the presidential associates and active alumni shared his Gomillion financial aid story with me, I learned that Dean Gomillion had given similar assistance to other students.

I also got some emergency help from Dean of Women Hattie S. West (later Kelly), an authoritative figure around campus who had been in the last Tuskegee high school class to graduate when Washington was president. I was nervously anticipating mail with funds to help me buy my meal ticket. When I checked in at the desk with the house adviser, she was rather snooty and refused to look for the mail. By now, readers know, I had an edge back then. I said, "I ought to reach across this desk and choke you." Of course, she reported me to the dean of women. I didn't get punished for that because I could obey in the ways that were important. I needed the money so I could buy my meal ticket. Dean West told me to not spend my cash on food as I went through the cafeteria line but to pay down the meal ticket with what I had and as money arrived.

When I wanted to go to summer school, my sister wrote to tell me that she had just been hired in a training program and had enough money to partially pay my fees. Dean West intervened when the head of the financial aid office refused to allow me to apply the funds, expressing skepticism that my sister would have a salary in a training program. He had made a hasty conclusion, not knowing she was being paid a full salary. I have forgotten his name, which is probably a good thing.

Dean West, on the other hand, was one of my saviors. She arranged for me to work in her office, where I filed and picked up the mail at the post office and distributed it to the other dorms. She also hired me to decorate her Christmas tree with all the Christmas cards that she had received. It was the first time I had done something like that, and I thought it quite neat.

My favorite teacher was Dr. Vernon McDaniel, who taught teacher education. I got my first and only college "Incomplete" grade from him. He did not stand in front of the class and lecture. That was a new experience for me. He said, "Why should I lecture to you from the book? You're supposed to read." When

I finally finished that class, I realize how important what he was telling us was and have carried much of it with me. He would say that anybody can be a good teacher, but you have to want to be a great teacher and add to the profession. He also used some of his growing-up experiences as object lessons. When he moved from the country to a larger community school, he was placed one grade back without being tested, although he had read more than a hundred books by the time he enrolled in that school. To assume that somebody from the country did not know anything was prejudiced. His looks caused people to think he was probably just a run-of-the-mill person instead of a college professor. Perhaps this kept him humble. He left us with a lot of sayings on everyday life to reflect on. He'd say, "If you like your streets clean, then you have to respect the people who clean it."

Dr. Frank Toland, a historian, probably conveyed the academic material that proved most stimulating in later life, although that would have been difficult to predict at the time. I had him at one o'clock, right after lunch. We left the cafeteria and went to Toland's class, the hardest class in which to stay awake. He would say, "This is Toland's classroom. This is not a hotel. So no sleeping in my class." I think the cadence of his speech made one sleepy also. In teaching the history of civilization, he went through all the stages. One day he asked me to grade some papers for him. Maybe he thought that if I saw what the other students did, then saw my grade, I would see my errors. It was multiple choice. I could have changed the ones I had wrong, but I would never consider doing that. I knew that I had some choices wrong and left it at that.

Memories of Toland and his torturous lessons came back to me in 2006, when two of my children and I went to China. Unlike most in our group, we were not there to study Chinese medicine and hence had a little more leisure time for exploration. We hired a driver, "Johnny Yellowcar," who picked us up at our hotel in Beijing and took us to the archaeological site where the Peking Man bones had been discovered. As I read the signage, I could hear Toland intoning. I have heard him other times in my travels, including a motorcoach tour around France where we passed signs for the caves that the Cro-Magnons occupied in the Dordogne. I got a chance to express some gratitude to Toland, albeit through his son, during my return to Tuskegee. We had started up a conversation with a young man working at the desk in the Carver Museum and learned he was Professor Toland's son. He told us his father was still teaching at Tuskegee. He had also been in the march to chapel that morning. I did not immediately recall seeing him, but looking back I realize that I had. Although it was too late to track down Professor Toland, I showed his son a photo from China, taken a year earlier

Lifting the Veil of Ignorance, statue by Charles Keck at Tuskegee University. The George F. Landegger Collection of Alabama Photographs in Carol M. Highsmith's *America.* Library of Congress, Prints and Photographs Division.

and still on my son's camera, and asked that he tell his father. It is a photo of me walking out of the remains of the Peking cave into a bright day.

During my days as a student, I did not fully understand how vital some faculty were to civil rights—McDaniel led a movement that got Black school teachers pay equity—or how committed they were to growth. Gomillion was working on his doctorate in sociology from Ohio State University while serving Tuskegee and fighting for civil rights. My connection to these leaders and the spirit of Tuskegee were rekindled throughout that visit around the campus, from Booker T. Washington's Oaks home down to the airfield where the Tuskegee Airmen trained.

As we left the chapel that day, the faculty and the other presidential associates and I headed for a photo shoot at the iconic Booker Washington Memorial, *Lifting the Veil of Ignorance,* where Washington is shown lifting a shroud covering a Black man holding a book (see photo 11). My children were eager to photograph me and themselves standing before the evocative sculpture. I have not shared with my children how I, on my graduation day in 1955, felt compelled to visit this spot while still wearing my cap and gown. Mama was not there; no family was. Although I married in my junior year, my husband was spending most of that time on a US Coast Guard cutter in Alaska. I was flooded with emotions as I made my way to the monument. Tears streamed down my face as I stood in front of it. I was sad, relieved, scared of what the future held. Lord, what do I do after this? I turned, wiped my tears, and walked the fifty yards back to my dorm.

eighteen

"THE ONE"

It would be a nice poetic flourish to say that on the night I met my husband-to-be, lyrics like "some enchanted evening" rang through my head. But that would be too much literary license. What really happened was that on one sweltering, summer evening, our eyes, mine brown, his hazel, met across a small room. He was seated in a chair beside a dresser, his blondish hair combed back in curly waves, his eyes observing me intently. I could say my heart skipped a beat, but that too would be an embellishment. However, a relative of mine did set the stage for what was an unusual courtship by today's standards.

My sister Mattie Mae, her husband, Norman Powell, and their two children, Roxie and Norman Jr. (Bubba), lived across the field from Joseph and Maggie Martin and their family in Cottageville, another small town in the county. Roxie and Bubba had adopted Aunt Mag and Uncle Joe as their very own and spent a lot of time with them. My sister Henrietta visited with Mattie's family for a week or two and returned home with Roxie and Bubba, and talking about the cute boy she met whom I just had to meet. She had, in her lifelong way of being a bit of a buttinsky, told him all about me. She said he told her, "She is the one I'm waiting for."

When we took Roxie and Bubba back home the next week, they were ready to go see Aunt Mag and Uncle Joe almost before they got out of the car. Henrietta was just as anxious for me to meet this cute boy. We were both sixteen.

After we met that summer of 1947, I left to work at Voorhees High School and Junior College over in Denmark, about thirty miles from Smoaks. My work on the campus helped to finance the upcoming school year. Later that year, I received a letter from Rutrell, who at age seventeen had joined the US Coast Guard. We wrote to each other over the years. He wrote that he knew from the minute we met that I would be his wife. Although I had no such dream at that time, six years after our first meeting, we were married (see photo 12).

We did not recite our own vows, but by that time I had read the Bible through three times, from Genesis to Revelation. It was from Ruth, my favorite

My wedding party. Left to right: Minnie Jenkins, my aunt; Kate Jenkins (Casley, her daughter and my cousin); Ruth Robinson Martin; Rutrell Martin; Fred "F. D." Douglas Robinson, my brother. August 23, 1953

book in the Bible, that I took "for whither thou goest, I will go; and where thou lodgest, I will lodge. Thy people shall be my people, and thy God, my God."

In fact, this had already become a reality. I came to know his family well during the six years after he and I met. I saw his family when I visited my sister's family. Rutrell's mother was a Creel, a popular surname of people descended from Native Americans in the area; they had their own area of Cottageville that was sometimes referred to as "Creeltown." I saw Rutrell only five times prior to his making his return trip from Alaska to New York for our wedding. Ours had been a courtship of letter writing. I followed him through his career moves from New York, to Seattle, and to New London, Connecticut, having six children and also building my own career. In the years when the children were quite young I ran the household myself for a few months at a time when he was out to sea. After Rutrell retired, he followed me to Florida when, after earning a doctorate in Connecticut, I got my first college teaching job in social work.

Ruth's words, "Where thou diest, will I die, and there will I be buried," were my sentiments when I chose a dual headstone when he died in 2005, following seventy-four days in and out of a coma following a massive stroke. He is interred along with my siblings in Lovely Hill Cemetery, where I too will join him in death.

nineteen

Finding Miss Barnes

Even as we got into our seventies, there was one teacher that my classmates and I recalled with much fondness. That was Miss Barnes. She was much admired by those who were in her fourth- and fifth-grade classes, as well as the other grades. As Justine said of her, "She had a way about things that you really appreciated. I wanted to be like Ms. Barnes." Thomas also named Miss Barnes as one of the teachers who motivated him to want to make something of himself.

Because she taught the fourth and fifth graders, she was not my teacher during her first year at our school, which was also the year that Johnsville and Simmons merged. My friend Virginia and F. D. were in her class while I was in the classroom for second and third graders. I was envious. Although I had some years to get through before I was in her class, two separate events provided me the opportunity to have regular contact with her. One was the Christmas program and the end-of-year school program, which she helped to organize; the second was when all girls met in her classroom one afternoon per week for home economics.

Despite our admiration for Miss Barnes, my classmates and I had not kept track of her, but during my interviews with classmates in the late 1990s, I had some special news to share.

In the 1970s I started work as a social worker in the Groton Public Schools in Connecticut, having recently earned a master's in social work (MSW). One of the teachers invited me to join a social club. The first meeting I attended, we all introduced ourselves. I was the only new woman, and naturally I got quizzed. A woman named Vernice and I were seated beside each other on the couch. When I announced that I grew up in Smoaks, South Carolina, Vernice said, "My first teaching job was in Smoaks."

"Where did you teach?"

"Smoaks Elementary School. There was only one school."

"Well, you couldn't have taught at my school," I said, initially thrown because she did not mention Johnsville-Simmons by name.

"The principal was Mr. Mason."

"There were only four teachers at my school. Miss Wakefield, Miss Walker, and my favorite teacher, Miss Barnes —."

"That was me," she said, interrupting me as I ticked off names.

"You can't be Miss Barnes. She was crazy about Mr. Mosley."

"That was me."

"My Miss Barnes had long hair and walked with a switch."

"That was me."

Soon we had both slid off the couch and were down on the floor, hugging each other, both talking at the same time. Needless to say, we kept interrupting the meeting that night to ask questions about each other. Mrs. Vernice Cook was my very own Miss Barnes. Her marriage to Cleophus Darrow Cook at age thirty brought her to New London, Connecticut, a similar path that I traveled with a husband in the military. And here's something else: Miss Barnes (Vernice Barnes Cook) was my oldest daughter's sixth-grade teacher at a school she briefly attended in New London, shortly after our move from Seattle in 1967.

Ironically, I had pulled the children out of that school within two months after they started because of the highly segregated school district lines that forced my children to walk by a predominantly white school to attend the predominantly Black school farther away. We arrived in Connecticut just a few weeks prior to the start of school. We walked over to the school to register and were surprised to be turned away with the news that we were in another school district. Sound familiar? That did not set well with me. We found housing in a different school district, albeit one where children of color were a minority, to finish out the school year. As a result, my reunion with Miss Barnes was delayed.

Miss Barnes came from a big family in Charlottesville, Virginia. Her parents, including a few of her siblings, came to visit her and stopped by the school several times. They were a good-looking bunch. Her father was ramrod thin, tall, and distinguished looking; her mother and siblings had light-brown complexions, appeared in good physical shape (not too fat, not too thin), and were all of good height, more than 5'7". Vernice was an attractive woman. Light-brown complexion, below-the-shoulder-length hair, and a well-proportioned figure. When we were reunited, I made sure I teased her about the walk she had back in our school days.

"I am sure you exaggerated as you, with your hands extended to your side, swept the sides of your dress as you switched your hips," I said. She laughed.

When I visited Vernice at her home in New London for an oral history interview in the late 1990s, I was able to pass along the regard with which my surviving classmates held for her. In 1981 I had attended the retirement party given for her and had mused, "How lucky I am to have been at the beginning of her teaching career and now at the ending of it."

I had another one of those small-world-after-all reunions with a teacher from South Carolina. I met Daisy Dawson, who had taught home economics at Harbison, at a PTA meeting in Seattle in the 1960s, striking up a friendship between our families that lasted until her death. The reunion with Miss Barnes was a little later, but because of her impact on me at such a young age, seeing her again felt more like the hand of destiny at work.

twenty

THE (POSSIBLY) TRAGIC FATE OF MR. SIX-TOE

We called him Mr. Six-Toe because we never knew him by name. We saw him just once. The day we met him, he took off his shoes and showed us his toes. He was born with the normal number of toes on one foot and six toes on the other. Neither F. D. nor I could recall which foot had the odd number when we discussed Mr. Six-Toe several years ago. Our young selves were quite amazed. He wiggled his toes around and around to make us laugh. Our family eventually moved into the home where he lived, but at the time I was too young to make the connection to him and the house. This is why the story I am going to share caused me to choke up when I heard it.

We were seldom told stories of violence; we mostly overheard our parents discussing them with other adults. These were often "hush, hush stories," whispered in low voices and never to be repeated. When Henrietta told me about the assumed fate of Mr. Six-Toe, I was too stunned to inquire further. The pain penetrated my every being so much that I wondered if I would open myself up to even more pain by asking further questions. By the time I digested the information and was ready for more, I didn't know anyone left who could or would tell the story.

It was a real shock when Henrietta said to me, shortly before she became ill and leading up to her death in 1995, "Listen, child, I need to tell you something." I don't remember what we were talking about. I knew it was important because she used that same solemn, serious voice with the same sober facial expression when we were boarding at school and she had to tell me we were out of food. She told the story, which she had heard from Doc Drain (Willie), in a jerky, unsteady voice as she fought to keep her emotions under control.

As Henrietta reported, someone heading to town stopped by and asked Mr. Six-Toe and his wife if they could bring anything back from the store for them. "Yeah," they responded. "We want us some shells 'cause we getting ready to kill us some white folk."

Right away, my hair stood on edge. "Were they out of their minds?"

The rest of the story is that the people brought the shells. Somehow some whites learned about it and considered it a threat. Later that night whites came, stuffed Mr. Six-Toe and his wife into the chimneys—one in each—built a fire in the two fireplaces, and burned them to death.

I never asked and Henrietta never told me whether Doc mentioned any conflict between Mr. Six-Toe and white folks. Regardless, why were they crazy enough to say such things to folks of any color or race? It was dangerous to say this to anybody out loud. Didn't they know that white folks lynched Blacks in South Carolina if they expressed any displeasure about anything? I don't even know if she knew all the details. I only know that as she told me this she was kind of like "shush, shush," as if she were still afraid to tell it.

Henrietta shared with me that Doc told her why the Drain family was not too happy when we moved into the home where Mr. Six-Toe once lived. First, I did not know there had been any animosity between the Drain family and ours when we moved in and when Papa subsequently bought the property. Second, it was the first knowledge I had that Mr. Six-Toe and family were related to the Drain family. Looking back, I realize I missed an important opportunity because I failed to ask Henrietta if she knew the name of Mr. Six-Toe and his wife.[1] I can only say that when my family moved into the house, my only thought as a ten-year-old was "My, how clean these bricks are! Even the hearth."

I am not sure how long Henrietta knew this story before she shared it with me. Perhaps she knew it and neglected to tell me because it was one of these sensitive matters that Blacks kept secret for fear of retaliation by whites. It was a serious flaw in southern culture, which allowed for such violent acts to occur. I did not question if it had happened. I knew from discussions I had overheard over the years that many a bad thing had happened. This one could have.

When Henrietta died in 1995, Madison was in a nursing home sharing a room with Doc Drain, who was in a wheelchair. It was the first time I had seen him in many years. He rolled his chair into a wall, unaware of his surroundings and unable to speak, so I never got to ask him further details about Mr. Six-Toe. Perhaps that was my sister's intention. As I write this story, I realize it is one I do not wish to face up close and personal because as I write, I still feel it in every nerve of my body. By the time my sister told me the story, the house was long since torn down. In fact, while it was still standing, Henrietta built Mother a more modern home approximately three hundred yards from it. Today, that house is also torn down, and we have sold the property. I should therefore be ready to put this haunting tale to rest.

Madison remained in the nursing home and occasionally was admitted to the hospital until his death in 2001. Doc's older sibling, Took, was in the hospital at this time, but he too was not well enough to be burdened with my curiosity.

I still consider the subject of Mr. Six-Toe an unsolved mystery. I did come up with one last idea in 2009. Nine Drain, Doc's brother who was one year younger than I, was still alive at that time. Perhaps he knew the answer. I telephoned F. D. and asked him, given that he still had contact with Nine, to please call him and ask him two questions. One, "What was the name of the man Took bought his home from?" Two, "What does he know about the Six-Toe man?" F. D. called me back within a half hour.

First, he told me that Nine had cancer and was not doing too well; however, he was able to talk, and his senses were intact. Nine never knew Mr. Six-Toe and the family who lived in our old house before we moved in. Nine did say that the white man who had sold the neighboring property to Took had a friend, another white man who used to visit, who was said to have commented, "Colored folks should all be ground up and used for fertilizer." Was that the fate of Mr. Six-Toe? It is one of those local southern mysteries that will likely never be revealed. I will leave this Earth among the last generation to have heard it and having seen enough to know that it could have happened.

twenty-one

"Something Good and Something Right"

As several incidents recounted in this book suggest, our family had a lot of contact with the Listons: doing trades, working on the farm, and sharing some leisure within the "rules" of our times. I have reflected on it quite a bit lately, pushed in part by questions from my children, who are curious about how such relationships worked with the racial codes of the segregated South as the backdrop. J. D. Liston was almost twenty years younger than my father, who was born in 1886. The Liston ancestors had owned slaves, according to a descendant who told me of doing research to confront the painful truth. Yet even as my father prospered, there was apparently not the kind of resentment that was reported in other areas of the South. Of course, we were Black, and the Listons were white, so the difference in status made us no real threat. The 1940 census indicates that my father reported income of $300 in 1939, the buying power of not much more than $4,000 in 2021, whereas J. D. Liston reported $500, and Ernest Connor reported $1,000, double the buying power of Liston in 2021 dollars but more than four times that of my father. Both white men owned well-built homes with household help; we were still renters at the time. Although the incomes reported cannot be verified and may be underreported for some neighbors, the census data provide a sense of the wealth gap.

For some time, my daughter Vivian, her journalistic curiosity not easily satisfied, kept pushing me with questions. She was particularly interested in knowing how some of the Listons might remember their time growing up in Smoaks, especially incidents such as the time Terry and Sunny Liston stood up to deflect the anger of some roughnecks who might surely have brought physical harm or worse on the day my cousin from the North appeared to have thrown a rock at their truck. Vivian kept pushing, but I would counter by suggesting the possible dangers of approaching whites in the South, how people might want the past to fade. But Vivian continued with her internet searches every now and then, alerting me when Sunny died. I was relenting a bit about contacting

Terry, recognizing how his voice might aid my memory, but then, in fall 2018, Terry died. By studying the condolences on the funeral home website, Vivian recognized the names of people both Terry and I had grown up with, including one of Ernest Connor's sons, James ("Jim"), then a ninety-two-year-old pediatrician and university researcher living in California. To my surprise, he agreed to talk. Prior to our conversation we exchanged memories through email about the names of the people living around the highway area. One of his grandchildren had been curious about the interactions between Blacks and whites and had done a video interview with him. Jim did not remember me. A few years older, he was a contemporary of my brothers, with whom he played baseball, although he had no immediate recollection of them.

The Connors were another Smoaks family with pre–Civil War planter roots. Jim said that when he was growing up, he did not have the conscious knowledge of many of the restrictions placed on Blacks, but spoke of coming to understand what the laws were and was sorry that Black schools and children did not get the money they were due. Although we shared landmarks and recalled the names of families living around us, his experiences were bound to be different. He said that he saw practices such as Blacks entering through the back door and whites not visiting Black homes as "custom" but had not interrogated it much beyond that. His friends outside of school were Black neighbors with whom he played games or hunted (he could still name some of them, including Charlie "Took" Drain). When asked about the racial animus associated with the times, including the racial epithets, he said he did not hear such views and words around his family.

He relayed that when he was young, he never understood why, around the same time each year, his uncle would talk over the fence and lend money to a Black farmer who lived nearby. Some months later, he'd see the Black man returning money. "I never realized why that was the case. Why would he come and borrow money from my uncle Frank?" Much later in life Connor came to understand: "We could get a loan from the banks, but they did not loan to Black people."

Connor was aware of how his father helped Black neighbors, including accompanying one woman to help her save property she was about to lose to merchant William Henry Varn. The stories about his father rang true because my family had borrowed money from Ernest Connor. I recall the young me being impatient once when my mother sent F. D. and me over to the Connors with a note asking to borrow money. Mr. Connor was having breakfast and finished reading the newspaper before he tended to our request.

Connecting with Jim Connor resulted in some exchanges with Ray Thomas, whose family had had much contact with mine. After Connor forwarded news of his contact with me, Thomas, who was still living in Smoaks, recalled trips to my father's mill. "I believe you are Joe and Beatrice Robinson's daughter," he said in a very warm email that addressed me as "Dr. Martin." It was his uncle, Luther, who had accepted the dollar down payment from my father, paving the way for the 113 acres we came to own. Thomas even made a trip to the courthouse to check a detail on the deed for me. At the beginning of this memoir, I wrote about Rommie Thomas's widow attempting to collect a debt that my parents proved had been paid. Rommie was Ray's uncle.

Some time ago, when Nine Drain (Johnny Lee) died of cancer, my brother F. D. attended the funeral and got in touch to tell me about who was there to say farewell to Nine. I was only mildly surprised when he told me about the Johnsville Hunters Club serving as pallbearers. Nine had always been an outdoor person with a love of hunting, fishing, and gardening. Medium-framed and standing about 5'10", he could be seen with a gun slung over his shoulder—that's if one got a chance to catch up to him. He hunted throughout deer season. F. D. told me about going down to Smoaks to pick up deer meat from Nine.

The biggest surprise about funeral participants came when he said, "Milton Thomas sang 'Precious Lord.'" Milton's father was Rommie Thomas, his mother the widow who mistakenly thought we owed her money.

How times have changed. Here was a white man, walking with a pronged-foot cane, hobbling up to the front of the church to sing at his Black friend's funeral. I knew they had been friends for years. Nine told me this in a telephone conversation back in 2006: "I see or hear from Mill three or four times a week."

The helpful reception from Jim Connor and Ray Thomas made me regret not making contact with Terry prior to his death. The conversation probably would have been more welcoming than I thought. In some ways we walked similar paths in our career. Terry earned a doctorate and became a school superintendent. Prior to earning my doctorate, I worked as a school social worker and had worked within similar school district bureaucracies. Although the Liston and Connor contemporaries started out with more advantages than I had, the level of education and professional accomplishments that at least three of us from that out-of-the-way patch of a town attained was amazing. My experience with Jim Connor, and Vivian's insistence, gave me the confidence in 2020 to contact Terry's son, Rallie Liston, a school superintendent in South Carolina. Rallie is a contemporary of my children. Right away, in his first response to my email, one could see once again how times have changed. The email began: "Miss Ruth (Dr. Martin)."

During a soul-stirring conversation, as we exchanged family stories, Rallie clearly enjoyed hearing the good memories I had of his father and grandfather. It was not uncomfortable as I pressed to try to understand what type of racial experiences might have been relayed from generation to generation. Rallie had never heard about the encounter with the men working on the highway, although he joked that throwing the rock seemed like something his father would have done. But Terry instilled in him a sense of respect across racial lines. Rallie shared how, when schools were integrated in their community and he was assigned to take a bus to a previously Black school, his father and mother never expressed resistance. Rallie said that while he was growing up, he noticed his father would get agitated when people expressed negative views around race. "I once said, 'Why are you so defensive?'"

His father responded: "You want people talking about your family? Boy, who do you think raised me?" As his father explained, he had been around Black people all his life. It made sense to the son.

The Listons maintained their connection to some Black people in Smoaks even after Terry built his life in other towns. For some years, Rallie's son hunted under the tutelage of Nine Drain. Our conversation felt like a blessing of sorts as we dipped into the past and discussed the successful lives we and our families built despite the backdrop of the Depression and segregation. We exchanged grateful emails in the following days. "You trusted my grandfather," Rallie wrote, seeming to want to confirm the conclusion he had taken from our conversation. We had both realized as we talked that the families along the highway shared many of the same values that had sustained generations. As Rallie had observed during that telephone call, "There was something good and something right along that road."

twenty-two

"Never to Come Up Anymore"

It was September 23, 2004, when my husband, our son Anthony, and I sat in a realtor's office in Walterboro, South Carolina. The business ahead of us was somber. We were there to discuss listing my share of property that had been in my family nearly all of my life. My father had officially closed the sale for the 113.5-acre farm in 1942. After the two house fires and other moves, we had finally moved into a house on a portion of that property in 1941.

For more than sixty-three years, it was our place called home. Henrietta built Mama a modern home to replace the four-room house around 1957, and Mama rented out the old house. It was where we would go when the world had beaten us down and we needed to heal. It was where we went when we were oh, so sad, and where we went to find joy. It was where we went after life had been cruel. It was where we went to visit our sick and to mourn our dead. As my brother Madison once said, "Nothing can make your feet feel so good as when you come home and put them in the South Carolina sand." My sister Henrietta chimed in, "You are so right, Matt." I could only give them an incredulous look. Nothing about sand in South Carolina or sand anywhere, for that matter, did I find enticing. What I remembered most about sand was that it could cut a painful slash across, under your toes, and that it took a while to heal. "Give me shoes!" I retorted. After leaving for college, I did not spend much extended time in South Carolina beyond some summers and visits when the children were young.

Our father once told us about the day in 1942 when he signed the contract to buy the house. He was in Walterboro with J. D. Liston and had the opportunity to buy the land, 113.5 acres, and needed a dollar to sign the contract. He located Liston, who was occupied elsewhere, and asked him to lend him a dollar. Liston did without questioning why he needed it. They had known each other for so many years that it hardly mattered. My father went back to the municipal building and closed the deal. Later, when my father told J. D. Liston about the deal, he was incredulous. "Had I known it was for sale I would have bought it myself."

Papa got a big laugh out of that. I am not sure if he was somewhat serious. The Listons owned much property of their own, including some abutting ours.

Less than five months before he passed away, Papa officially bought the 113.5 acres from W. L. (Luther) Thomas for $1,200. It stayed intact for decades, and putting my final portions up would mean the end of that connection. After signing the paperwork and leaving the realtor's office, the three of us drove to the cemetery at Lovely Hill Baptist Church in Smoaks. I needed to tell my siblings, especially Henrietta and Madison, of my decision.

"It is time," I said. Henrietta and Madison, three other siblings, and my father are buried there; somehow I felt the dead could hear me. It was particularly important for Madison and Henrietta to understand because my father took to his sickbed shortly after the bill of sale, and it was they, my brother Fred, my mother, and I who worked the land and paid off the mortgage. I also stopped by Green Pond Memorial Cemetery and told my mother about the impending sale. It was she who ended up working her fingers to the bone to hold on to this property.

The winter after my father's death my mother took to her bed. She was very weak, and her face was all drawn. Pitiful is how I saw her. She was in bed when we left for school in the morning and still there when we returned from school in the afternoon. We never knew exactly what her illness was. Now, with professional insight, I would diagnose her as depressed. She lingered in her bed until one spring day when we returned from school and she was in the field piling the huge cotton stalks that had failed to rot. To see her back out there, using up her energy, frightened my brother and me, but she assured us she was all right. She had even put sweet potatoes in the oven, and they had baked. Sweet potatoes have always been one of my favorite foods, and this day I was delighted.

Today, I can still see my mother working in the field and coming home for lunch to take a break away from the stifling heat. She lay on the porch as we swatted gnats away while she tried to grab a little rest. "Mash my back for me," she would ask one of us. Sometimes, it would be F. D. or me who would press along her lower back with our hands or walk on her back and try to relieve her pain. She always seemed to have such bad backaches. Sometimes the expression in her eyes was so forlorn, tired, and haunted because she feared losing the land. I don't think she was ever free of worrying about it.

As I went through Mother's old papers, I realized part of the reason for her depressed mood. I saw papers upon papers showing how she borrowed money against the farm to keep it going. Notes and chattel mortgages abound to the Southern Fertilizer and Chemical Company until her death in 1964. One mortgage was recorded on March 20, 1961, and was due on September 15, 1961. This mortgage was for $263, for which Mother agreed to grant, bargain, and sell to Southern "5 ½ acres of cotton; 15 acres of corn; 1 red-spotted sow and increase [any pigs that the sow might have had during that period]; 1 white and black male hog; 2 acres of cucumbers; and 2 acres of peanuts." The mortgage was recorded as paid on November 1, 1961.

Reading it today, I cried for my mother. Here she was mortgaging everything she stood to earn from her crops. She was over sixty-three years old and still had to struggle every day to eke out a living on this farm. With all of its hard work and sacrifices, Mama would not have left that farm, though, for anything. To her, it was home, and she never had the urge to leave it, even if it were to make easier living. She stayed there when she remarried, a few years before she died. A few days before her death, she said that she caught cold when she had gone down to the ditch row. It was years before I realized the ditch row was a ditch the government cut through the properties to drain water off the land.

In earlier receipts that were dated September 23, 1948, I saw how difficult it was for Mother to hold on to this property. The receipts were for seed tickets. These were seeds from the cotton that had been taken to the gin. The seeds' net pounds sold at $65.00 per ton, and the gross pay was $28.92, with $7.02 deducted for ginning, bagging, and ties. Her net was $21.90. The second bale netted even less, $15.41. Years after Mother passed, we sold the timber off the land and earned thousands of dollars. Why, I wondered as I looked through the papers, didn't Mother sell the timber? It could have made her financial situation much easier. And, no, I couldn't handle it without shedding tears. One might ask me, "Then why sell?" I would answer that it was because of the same compelling force that drove me away in the first place.

There was just no opportunity there. No real freedom. Going back often confirmed my reasons for leaving. It was an everyday challenge living in the South. Some rules caused me to gnash my teeth or to smile when I considered doing so a waste of good energy. I could not have felt it more than the summer of 1962 when my husband flew from Seattle with our four children and me to spend the summer with Mama, who was sick. He left us to return to his ship in Seattle, saying, "Take care of yourself and the children."

I knew it was going to be difficult taking care of the children, looking after my mother, and, most of all, adhering to a culture that required one to say "Yes, ma'am" and "No, ma'am" to white folks. I braced for a long summer.

My first test came when visiting my mother in the hospital. My sister, Mattie Mae, spent nights sitting up in the hospital with Mama while I stayed with our children. She was combing Mama's hair when a nurse came in: "Oooh, I just love your gray hair! It reminds me of how I used to love to sit on my mammy's lap and play in her hair. He-he-he." That did not conjure up any image I cared to remember.

Mattie Mae smiled ever so sweetly and said, "Oh, yes, ma'am." That tense moment passed as quickly as it had begun.

On another trip to the doctor with Mama, we were waiting in the "colored" waiting room. We waited, waited, and waited. My six-month-old had cried while holding her ear most of the night. We silently complained to each other with our eyes. I was thinking, "When have I heard this before?" I remembered it had been years before I left the South and when F. D., having had a toothache, waited all week until he got to Branchville on Saturday to have his tooth extracted. The dentist gave him a Novocain shot to dull the pain. He waited and waited. The Novocain wore off. Finally, all of the dentist's white patients had left. His phone rang. "Oh," he said, "I forgot. I still have a nigger in here I have to see." He came and worked on the tooth without benefit of new Novocain. When F. D. came home, he described the pain he felt: "I was so insulted. Had I not been in such pain with the tooth, I would have left without him seeing me."

On that day in 1962, we had been waiting all morning. "I am going straight into that white waiting room and demand that he see us now!" I announced. Mattie and her son, Norman Junior, grabbed me, one by each arm and held me back. They and Mom pleaded with me to remain calm. "Aunt Ruth, you will only make Grandmamma worse if something happens to you. The police are bound to beat you up and take you to jail."

"I am feeling OK. I can wait," Mama pleaded.

"Think of what will happen to your children," Mattie implored.

They finally talked me down just as a policeman poked his head in the door of the waiting room. "Anything wrong?"

"No suh, no suh," chimed Mattie Mae and Norman Jr.

We finally got into the doctor's office. He took good medical care of Mama and Sonya, my baby, who had an ear infection.

Mattie explained to him, "I thought it might be, but I didn't have any drops to put in her ear."

"Had you done that, she would have gone deaf," the doctor advised.

My good feelings about how this incident ended were overshadowed by how badly things ended. Two years later, my mother made a visit to another doctor. This time, she waited in a car while the doctor went to have his lunch. The doctor returned in time to pronounce her dead. I was in Seattle when the telephone call came from Henrietta.

"Ruth, listen, I need to tell you something."

On August 4, 2006, the last section of my property was sold. The check arrived in Connecticut through overnight mail. I looked at the check and knew this money would not be used for silly pleasures. It would be spent to purchase another house with the hope that any proceeds from my mother's hard work would be put to a good cause. It was with this plan in mind that I deposited every dime and kept it until I used it toward a down payment on a spacious family home with my children's blessing. Rutrell, my husband, had died in 2005. It was my hope that if any of my six children needed a place to hang out, get together, experience solitude, or have an old-fashioned homecoming, they would feel this was home.

I can say this of the aims of Beatrice's ledger: Mission Accomplished. Obstacles overcome, dreams realized. All checks and balances, weights and measures, accounts received and accounts paid. Mama often wrote a statement when a bill was paid, and it feels right to use it now: "Settlement, never to come up any more."

EPILOGUE

It had been a fitful night weighed down by sadness as I lay awake thinking that the good times would end for me. I had spent four nights in a hospital in Florence, Italy, where I was living with my son and daughter, who was teaching there for a month. Our Airbnb was right off the Piazza Duomo, just yards from Cattedrale Santa Maria di Fiore (Il Duomo), the transfixing medieval structure and the uncompromising bells of Giotto's tower, which greeted us each morning. I had been a tourist in Italy before, but with our daily routines I was becoming part of everyday Florence even as I cursed the lack of salt in bread (a tradition dating back to a war between Florence and Pisa hundreds of years ago).

We had taken a bus trip to a wine tasting and visited Sienna the prior weekend, and I was still trying to recuperate a week later. In Italy, of course, there is also the heat, but I am always cold when others are too hot. Although our apartment was wired for individually controlled air conditioning, I had ordered it shut down in my room. I was feeling uncomfortable, a little dizzy at times, and started seeing odd figures in my peripheral vision. The pills my US doctor had prescribed for some bronchial aggravation taken on top of my other meds seemed to be the culprit. I stopped taking them after a couple of days and just sought rest.

The next thing I recall is waking up in the emergency room at Santa Maria Nuova, just a couple of blocks from our apartment. The doctors said I had had a ministroke. My daughter and son had gone out to take a quick look inside a nearby shop that specialized in highly crafted Pinocchio figures, which I had been hoping to purchase prior to our departure in a few weeks. They were gone for less than an hour, stopping to bring in some paninis for lunch. When they got home, they found me unconscious. After a mad dash for emergency services, a telephone call expedited with help from the owner at the restaurant next to our building, an ambulance crew worked on me for close to forty-five minutes. Four nights in a hospital where people don't speak your language is frightening, but the medical staff took care of the "tourista" without any of the insurance hassles one has in the United States even when medical workers speak your language.

The girl from Smoaks on
the Great Wall of China,
November 2006.

That summer of 2017 was not the first night I had spent in a foreign hospital. In 2009, on a tour through Israel, where we saw wonders from the Weeping Wall to Gethsemane to the Sea of Galilee, which we sailed, I fell at one of the archaeological sites and spent the night in Hadassah for observation. We had just been there hours earlier to see the Chagall stained glass windows. On that night my two daughters sat up in the hospital room, but we were out the following morning in time to go with our group to Masada and float in the Dead Sea later in the day. The hospital stay in Florence was much grimmer. I had never been unconscious before. One morning on a Nile cruise, I had awakened barely able to get up and spoke in a barely decipherable monotone, but orange juice spiked my apparently too-low blood sugar, and I was normal again. Florence was more frightening for all of us; my daughter began communicating with doctors and family in the United States, and we waited nervously. I am told I came back on my own just as the doctor was about to give me a stroke-reversal medication that could have caused damage even as it could also have helped.

One of my daughters and her husband arrived on a scheduled visit to Florence just hours after my stroke; my son and his teenage daughters came in for a planned vacation a few days after my daughter and son-in-law left. Alone at night in the hospital, I had too much time with my thoughts, too many hours to think it all was ending. I began scribbling notes for this Epilogue. Even as I struggled with my sadness, I also knew I was blessed. This Black girl from Smoaks had made it around the world, from South Africa, where I conducted oral histories with apartheid activists, to China (see photo 13), through Europe, and much of the United States, crisscrossing a few times. As I rethink some of my foreign travels, which have become such a big part of my life in the last two decades, I realize that I have probably added some other health scares or dramas to the list. I am nothing if not a trouper. I climbed the ranks of academia, published serious research, developed future social workers, and in my social work days helped many children and families. As the wife of a career serviceman, I spent months each year raising the children while my husband was at sea. I have given birth to thriving descendants: my six children, grandchildren, and great-grandchildren. We just hit the third generation of PhDs in the family. I am one of two surviving members of that graduating ninth-grade class in 1946. My brother F. D., my last surviving sibling, passed in 2018. Nearly all of my cousins are gone.

In the late 1990s I interviewed three classmates from my ninth-grade class of 1946 and touched base with the other three who survived. During the interviews we shared reflections on our lives and how we were able to thrive despite difficulties and a world that was often hostile. How did we do it? How did we overcome? Thomas Warren, a former New York subway conductor who returned to South Carolina after retirement, spoke of the "obedience" we showed authority: "You remember the teachers would have switches in the classroom and would whip you, and then send a note to your parents, and you better take that note home." But as Thomas also recalled, the teachers were dedicated "and started each day with a prayer." Faith and religion were important to our lives. Thomas, who attended Lovely Hill, the same church as I, said that the church deacons and other prominent figures played a big role in helping set the course: "To think about them, these were true leaders during that time. I guess you might say it was a different time. If they were doing anything, the younger generation didn't know it. They carried themselves in such a way that children respected them as role models and younger children wanted to be like them."

Two of the classmates I interviewed, Redell Stokes Fields, now the other surviving classmate, and Justine Stephens McCants, spent their careers as educators. The value of education and the family support that pushed us to it were big themes in our conversation. We'd grown up with brothers and male relatives who were tied to the farm for a family's survival, which sometimes meant that it was the women in our generation who went away to school, leaving the men to work the farm. This was support that kept us going.

Epilogue

Looking over the stories I have shared throughout this book, I know a lot of personal spunk also pushed me through. My children, in reading about certain incidents, chuckle over the dean of women at Voorhees describing me and another woman as the "meanest girls" to come out of Smoaks. Had I had less fight, I would not have ended up where I did.

Mostly, I was blessed to have Joe and Beatrice Robinson as parents.

Postscript

The day after a draft of this book was submitted to the editor, Ruth Robinson Martin, my mother, suffered a small stroke, and then a bigger stroke a few days later while in the hospital. The 2020 incidents, just days before Christmas, were more damaging than the 2017 event in Italy she writes of here. She lost movement on her left side, and the strokes impaired some speech and other daily activities. Having lost most of her eyesight during the year prior, when COVID-19 resulted in physicians such as her eye doctor granting fewer appointments, she has had to deal with losses and move toward a new normal. I have worked with her to complete the book, which she started writing in a memoir-writing class more than fifteen years ago, shortly after my father died and after several years of interviews and other information gathering in the 1990s. She has been able to participate more on some days than others, but I am always surprised by her continued recall of people and scenes she relays in this book, as well as her memories of the travels we have shared.

At ninety and making plans for a ninety-first birthday party (God willing), my mother is not only among the ever-dwindling members of a generation, but she is also among the few African Americans left from her era who grew up in Smoaks, South Carolina. Her siblings are gone, as are most relatives her age, and just one classmate from Johnsville-Simmons, where she attended K through 9, survives. The passing of most people she knew made it all the more important for her to tell this story. How people lived, how they sought education, how they persevered despite harsh realities are all important pieces of history not so widely known. We are familiar with the stories of African American pioneers, of civil rights leaders and people in the forefront of those fights. Much less is known about the everyday life of the African Americans of my mother's generation who, with the support of family, Black educators, and institutions such as the church, were able to advance in America. Too often, the African American story is presented as one of struggle and dysfunction. The problems of the most unfortunate are treated as the defining portrait for all of Black America. I grew up knowing that my mother and her peers had overcome obstacles and built a foundation for my generation and those younger, but it was not until I delved into this project, helping with some contextual research, learning more about high and low moments of her family's life, that I was able to digest and understand what my parents and theirs overcame. These experiences are important for other Americans to understand, including younger African Americans without the benefit of looking back across generations to see that we have been a successful people for a long time in America.

As a journalism professor whose career started as a newspaper reporter, I had a number of questions about events in the manuscript that my mother could not answer. Always, I asked too many questions. She'd get a little impatient. I understood that she lived in a complicated space with many written and unwritten rules, but I had many questions about how Blacks and whites encountered one another in everyday life. We would hear stories about J. D. Liston, who lived nearby and was in my mother's life, or references to Ernest Connor, who appears to have been generous with neighbors.

The stories were somewhat different than the open hostility I assumed. I felt that part of the story she would be telling was about these small-town interactions between Black and white, something more complex than the racial violence in movies and other storytelling. All of the harshness was there, of course, but there was another layer of cooperation (not sure I would say community, as Blacks and whites did appear to belong to separate communities). As I discovered when I fact-checked just to keep names straight, many of the white families around during my mother's time were connected through marriage, and then there are white Rishers and Black Rishers, white and Black Hiers, and Stokes, moving in parallel lives. What did people make of that and the history that brought all of those connections about? That was definitely more than what my mother was going for. But the families in the 1940 census, who lived up and down the road, would factor into the story she would tell. My mother resisted dipping into the past to piece some of that story together, but she too came to see how some of the pieces fit and included some interviews with people connected to the white community. Smoaks along that stretch of highway would disappear from historical memory, including the local memory, but for her work.

My mother is a natural storyteller. It is testament to her ability that I was able to draw on some stories we heard growing up (more than a few times) to help her tease out ideas for this project. It does not claim to be a comprehensive rendering. With renewed efforts to suppress voting rights and other racial inequities so prominent today, it was natural to seek recollections of any stories related to these struggles. But such incidents, such as the state of voting in Smoaks during her day, are not part of my mother's repertoire. Political talk, at least in a form an adolescent would have recognized, was not daily discourse. Even when Ray Thomas, a white lifelong resident of Smoaks, recalled that my mother's older sister, Mattie Mae, worked at the polling place at his church, this was news to my mother. With her own concerns as a young person and her time boarding away at school, my sense is such matters were not on her radar. The strength of her stories here is that she stuck to what she knew and experienced. My reporter's instincts are not completely satisfied, but perhaps the leads here will increase understanding for other projects.

What she did accomplish here was to tell the story of people who were extraordinary in their ability to survive and do better for the next generation. Recently, as I was talking with my mother about how remarkable it was that her mother was able to come up with a new plan for her to attend high school away from home each year, she paused—her post-stroke impairments produce slower speech—and then said, "Mama was always planning ahead." I did not know my mother's father, who died when she was young, but I did experience my grandmother, Beatrice. When I was about three, a younger sibling and I stayed with her for a few months. My most vivid memory is of her calling a neighbor to come shoot a snake that was in the front yard. Although she died while I was young (and one sibling not even yet born), Beatrice's sayings and favorite poems were passed on to my siblings and me through my mother. But we inherited more than that. The debts she listed in her ledger and her sacrifices to pay them made a better life for all of us who came after her. "Not to come up any more," she'd write in her ledger of debts as they were paid. Oh, but not forgotten.

Vivian B. Martin with Ruth R. Martin
Hartford, Connecticut
August 2021

Notes

two: Smoaks

1. The name issue and early settlement are explored in histories of Colleton County and family-published materials: Evelyn McDaniel Frazier Bryan. *Colleton County, S.C.: A History of the First 160 Years, 1670–1830*. (Jacksonville, FL: The Florentine Press, 1993); W. W. Smoak, *Historical Outline of Colleton County*, radio address and pamphlet (1933?); Neil A. Smoak, *The Smoak, Smoke, Rauch Family* (Dallas: 2001).

2. "Local Educator Redell Fields Turns 90," *Walterboro Live*, October 21, 2020, https://walterborolive.com/stories/local-educator-redell-turns-90,33055?

3. John Belton O'Neall, *The Negro Law of South Carolina* (Columbia, SC: J.G. Bowman, 1848), retrieved July 10, 2020, https//loc.gov/item/10034474.

4. Terence Finnegan, *A Deed So Accursed: Lynching in Mississippi and South Carolina* (Richmond: University of Virginia Press, 2013).

5. *Times and Democrat* (Orangeburg, SC), June 15, 1909, 4; June 19, 1909, 4.

five: Meeting the Drains

1. The Slave Relics Museum in Walterboro has closed.

six: School Days

1. *Public Schools of South Carolina: A Report of the South Carolina Education Survey Committee* (Nashville, TN: Division of Surveys and Field Services, George Peabody College for Teachers, 1948).

2. James Anderson, *Education of Blacks in the South, 1860–1935* (Chapel Hill: University of North Carolina Press, 1988).

3. African Americans were disproportionately affected by the decades-long battle against tuberculosis. In 1936 the Tuberculosis Association, as quoted by a Black newspaper in the state, indicated that African Americans made up a quarter of the twenty thousand tuberculosis deaths the prior year ("Tuberculosis among Negroes a Striking Problem," *Palmetto Leader*, May 23, 1936). Sanitariums, the facilities for the treatment of tuberculosis, had a limited number of beds and were restricted to whites through much of the crisis, although there were efforts to provide segregated spaces for Blacks. The *Palmetto Leader*, a newspaper published in Columbia from 1925 to 196?, provided ongoing coverage of conferences, held essay contests to increase awareness, promoted tuberculosis Christmas Seals (November 30, 1940), and made other efforts to increase tuberculosis prevention

among Blacks in South Carolina. A college essay contest, "What Negroes Should Know About Tuberculosis," announced in the *Palmetto Leader* on April 4, 1936, offered prizes of $10, $5, and $3, and it allowed winners to advance to a state contest. See https://historic newspapers.sc.edu/lccn/sn93067919.

4. R. R. Martin, "Rev. McTeer: A Teacher for All Times," *Mediaworks for the Community* 2, no. 5 (September/October 1993): 15.

eight: The Root Doctor

1. The most infamous Dr. Buzzard is believed to have been Stephany (sometimes spelled Stepheny) Robinson, whose exploits are detailed in "Dr. Buzzard," an entry in the *South Carolina Encyclopedia,* retrieved August 8, 2021, www.scencyclopedia.org/sce /entries/dr-buzzard. In this video a writer claims to have located Dr. Buzzard's grave: www.youtube.com/watch?v=5gARnIKrlA4.

thirteen: The German POW Occupation

1. Deann Bice Segal, *The German POWs in South Carolina: The Enemy among Us* (Lewiston, NY: Edwin Mellen, 2005). The proper term for the airbases was "army airfield" or "army airbase," which Segal uses in appendix 2. Coronaco Army Airfield was located in Greenwood. Charleston POE stands for Charleston Port of Entry. Walterburo was Segal's spelling in that section of her book.

2. J. Todd Moye, *Freedom Flyers: The Tuskegee Airmen of World War II* (Oxford, UK: Oxford University Press, 2012).

3. See "Enterprise Bank Celebrates 100 Years," *Times and Democrat,* April 11, 2020, https://thetandd.com/news/local/enterprise-bank-celebrates-100-years/article_970fdfc0 -a9c2-5005-ba6c-8a2fbe4ebb55.html.

4. Sherry J. Cawley, *Around Walterboro South Carolina* (Charleston, SC: Arcadia, 1998).

seventeen: Tuskegee

1. Gomillion v. Lightfoot, 364 U.S. (339) 1960, https://supreme.justia.com/cases /federal/us/364/339.

twenty: The (Possibly) Tragic Fate of Mr. Six-Toe

1. I have some memory that Mr. Six-Toe was named Tom Brown and his wife was Rachel Jean, the alleged root doctor who visited our home when I was young. One night as I mulled this over, after some questioning from my daughter Vivian, who was attempting to find documents regarding Mr. Six-Toe, Doc Drain appeared to me in a dream and asked, "Is there something you want to ask me?" If there was anyone who would have known the answer to the identity of Mr. Six-Toe, it would have been Doc Drain, now deceased, who was related to him in some way. I did not recall the dream after waking, but at some point I did tell Vivian that Mr. Six-Toe was Tom Brown and that his wife was Rachel Jean. Later, Vivian noted that I had referenced Rachel Jean and her husband in my chapter on root doctors and wondered if these were the same people or jumbled memory. I was five or six when they visited and am not certain of what I knew of them

at the time; the alleged murders would have happened several years later. Because of the lack of documents and the lack of remaining people with firsthand information, I can't say for sure. But the story is out there now.

Index